How to Analyze People

Instantly Learn Body Language, Social Skills, and Secret Techniques that Psychologists and FBI Agents Use to Read People

Written By Beto Canales & Habits of Wisdom

© Copyright 2019 Beto Canales & Habits of Wisdom - All rights reserved.

The content contained within this book may not be reproduced, duplicated or transmitted without direct written permission from the author or the publisher.

Under no circumstances will any blame or legal responsibility be held against the publisher, or author, for any damages, reparation, or monetary loss due to the information contained within this book. Either directly or indirectly.

Legal Notice:

This book is copyright protected. This book is only for personal use. You cannot amend, distribute, sell, use, quote or paraphrase any part, or the content within this book, without the consent of the author or publisher.

Disclaimer Notice:

Please note the information contained within this document is for educational and entertainment purposes only. All effort has been executed to present accurate, up to date, and reliable, complete information. No warranties of any kind are declared or implied. Readers acknowledge that the author is not engaging in the rendering of legal, financial, medical or professional advice. The content within this book has been derived from various sources. Please consult a licensed professional before attempting any techniques outlined in this book.

By reading this document, the reader agrees that under no circumstances is the author responsible for any losses, direct or indirect, which are incurred as a result of the use of information contained within this document, including, but not limited to, — errors, omissions, or inaccuracies.

Table of Contents

Introduction 8
    Pay Close Attention to Nonverbal Cues 11
    Concentrate on Your Tone When Speaking ... 12
    Maintain Eye Contact 13

Chapter 1: The Psychology Behind Reading Body Language 15
    What is Body Language? 16
    The Importance of Body Language 18
    Origin of Humans and Body Language 19
    How to Read Body Language 20

Chapter 2: The Significance of Learning and Understanding Non-verbal Communication 34
    Factors Affecting Understanding of Body Language 36

Chapter 3: Principles of Body Language 41
    Basic Tips on Body Language 44
    How to Read People's Body Language 49

Chapter 5: The Language Differences in Sexes . 62
    Men's Body Language 63
    Female Body Language 71

Chapter 6: Benefits of Knowing How to Read Body Language and Facial Expressions 80

    Enhance Parenting Skills 81

    Give Good Impression in Job Interviews 82

    Nourish Personal Relationships 83

    Identify and Read Negative Nonverbal Behavior..83

    Project Yourself Positively 86

    Facial Profiling 88

    Hair..92

    Eyebrows 94

    Eyes... 100

    Nose 103

    Cheeks.. 105

    Lips 106

    Identifying Personality Types 111

Chapter 7: Learning, Recognizing, and Reading Hidden Body Messages.................................... 147

    Knowing When Someone is Lying 150

    Reading People on a Date 154

    Communicating Effectively in an Interview 156

    Reading Power Cues.................................... 160

Chapter 8: Knowledge and Techniques Required to Understand and Interpret Body Language . 163

   How Body Language is Connected to Emotional Quotient (EQ) 163

   Ways to Gauge EQ Through Body Language 169

Chapter 9: Reading and Understanding Different Cues 175

   Emotional Cues 183

   Attraction Cues 185

   Relational Cues 188

Chapter 10: Understanding Non-Verbal Cues for Success in Career and Business 193

   Microexpressions to be Aware of When Negotiating 193

   Reading Body Language to Win Negotiations 199

   Body Signals to Look for in a Negotiation .. 200

   Signs that You Have the Other Person's Full Attention 208

   Tell-Tale Signs of Disagreement 209

Chapter 11: Is Faking Body Language Possible? 212

   Microexpressions 213

Chapter 12: Training Exercises to Improve Body Language 218

Body Language Exercises (Solo) 219
Body Language Exercises (Group Activity) .224
Conclusion..244

Introduction

Have you ever wanted to know when people are telling lies or know the real intention of a romantic interest? It can be quite depressing to not get a deal because you didn't know what went through your client's head.

Almost everyone has experienced some dilemma in one way or another because their instincts weren't strong when needed or simply because they didn't listen to their gut and did otherwise.

This isn't about your gut or instinct, but one thing is for sure. You want the ability to READ PEOPLE LIKE A BOOK!

This sounds incredibly impossible but NOT ANYMORE! Read this book and you'll find out how amazing it is to read someone, detect lies, and learn more about your romantic interests.

How would you want to perfectly close a deal simply by guessing a client's next reactions and knowing what tickles him?

Body language refers to nonverbal signals we use when we are communicating with other people. These nonverbal signals make up a large part of our daily communications. Though we are thinking that we effectively convey our message using words, it could be surprising to learn that our body movements and facial expressions - things we don't actually say can convey more volumes of information than those we convey through words.

Let's take this for an illustration. A frown can indicate sadness or disapproval while a smile is a sign that the person is happy or approves of whatever it is that is being presented. In most cases, our facial expressions reveal our inner feeling while in a particular situation. However, verbal and nonverbal communication can sometimes be contradicting. In this case, it is more useful if you know how to decipher the person's nonverbal cues and signals than merely rely on their words. This can be especially true when you are negotiating for a deal, dealing with a cheating partner, or taking a crucial job interview.

There are also times when you can get away from a lurking danger because you can read danger cues of charming strangers or save yourself from embarrassment because you were able to reverse the situation even before others recognize it.

An expression on a person's face can help us determine if we can trust or believe what they are saying. There is one study that revealed that the most trustworthy facial expression bears a slight smile with a slight raise of the eyebrows.

By learning the skill of reading body language and micro expressions, you will be able to:

- Understand the meaning behind a person's body language
- Read people's thoughts before they even speak out
- Analyze personality through body language cues

- Know when your partner is cheating on you
- Detect when someone is telling a lie
- Identify positive and negative body signals

Learning a strong communication skill can help you in both your personal and professional life. While verbal communication is important, it constitutes less than 50% of your daily interpersonal communication.

So, how can you improve your nonverbal communication?

Pay Close Attention to Nonverbal Cues

People communicate information in a number of ways. You need, therefore, to pay attention to the following:

- Eye contact
- Body movements
- Posture
- Gestures

- Tone of voice

All of these signals convey important data that aren't put into words. By paying attention to these unspoken behaviors, you can likewise improve your own ability to communicate nonverbally.

Spot Incongruent Behaviors

If a person displays nonverbal behaviors that don't match their words, pay extra attention. Would you believe someone telling you they're happy when a frown cuts deep across their face?

When someone says something that greatly contradicts their body language, it's useful to pay close attention to these subtle cues.

Concentrate on Your Tone When Speaking

Your own tone of voice carries a myriad of information especially of emotions on varied intensities. Notice you others respond to your tone of voice and try to use it in emphasizing ideas to want to communicate across.

If you are trying to show genuine interest on what someone is telling you, you can express your enthusiasm with an animated tone of voice. This will not only convey your own feelings about what is being relayed but likewise generate interest in people listening to you.

Maintain Eye Contact

Good eye contact is another significant nonverbal communication skill you need to develop. Without eye contact, the person you are talking to may feel you're uncomfortable with them or hiding something which can emit a negative feeling. On the other hand, using too much of this, you can appear to be intimidating or confrontational.

While you need to use eye contact in communicating, it is also important to learn that good eye contact is not necessarily fixing your stares on someone's eye.

Learning how to read body language will tell you all the difference between negative and positive body movements, expressions, and gestures and how they affect other people as well.

Chapter 1: The Psychology Behind Reading Body Language

We always hear people say action speaks louder than words - the impact even of a passive action is sure to hit you more than words can say.

Words unspoken are subtly exhibited through body language and some studies suggest that it constitutes more than 60 percent of what a person is trying to communicate. Learning to read and analyze unspoken words through nonverbal cues is, therefore, a skill that is valuable and beneficial. It carries a myriad of benefits. It could help you avoid possible danger or it could help someone else in need.

Have you ever heard of an abducted youth who was saved by law enforcement because the security guard of the condominium where her or she was kept was able to quickly read body language? Yes, reading body language and the facial expressions of a person can save a life!

How a person rolls their eyes or how facial expressions change can reveal what a person is thinking or hiding inside. Even a smile can have many variations. It can be sweet one or could be an evil smirk. You just have to be quick enough to identify expressions to know if a person's smile conveys pleasure or actually something in contrast.

However, before we go much further, let's define what body language is.

What is Body Language?

Body language is a type of nonverbal communication where physical behaviors are utilized to convey information relating to thoughts and feelings of the individual who may or may not be consciously relaying the message. Such behaviors include eye movement, body posture, gestures facial expressions, touch, or even the use of space.

Simply put, body language is the unspoken element of communication that our mind is using to reveal our real emotions. If we are conscious of our body language, we can adjust it to project a more positive personality.

When talking about body language, we consider the subtle cues we are sending and receiving nonverbally. To get started, we can break it into different channels.

Knowing how to read micro-expressions is significant in understanding nonverbal behavior. There are seven universal micro-expressions that are seen on a person's face based on the emotions being experienced. It is difficult to fake a micro-expression.

This is a term used to refer to our body movement in a certain space. Basically, it is the study of space and how we relate to it - how we are more or less comfortable in a certain space.

These refer to all extensions of our body including hairstyles, jewelry, clothes, and accessories. How we act and go about with our ornaments tells more about us. Are you constantly touching your hair? Do you love wearing strong colors or a scent? These are all body cues that tell more about your personality and behavior. They are your body language.

The Importance of Body Language

In the 1960s, Albert Mehrabian conducted a study on the significance of gestures and intonations for conveying a certain message and the result showed that 7 percent of communication is verbal or with the use of words. Thirty-eight percent is paraverbal (use of tone and intonation) but 55 percent is nonverbal!

If armed with this knowledge, no one can keep a secret from a person who knows how to read these signs. If you have this skill, you can be good at playing poker, negotiating a deal, cross-examining a suspect, or catching a cheater. You can do and use a lot more of these to your advantage. The study may disclose everything, but the point is words are not enough to convey or understand a message. However, being able to read people like an open book will really put you at an advantage in almost all situations. Seeing a person's strengths and weaknesses in plain view will always give you a head start.

Origin of Humans and Body Language

The origin of body language goes back to the prehistoric time when men were not aware of their ability to communicate through verbal language. They only communicated via the sign language.

Some of these nonverbal signals are universal. Everyone can easily understand when someone is happy through the smile on their face. Agony is expressed when in pain - physical or emotional while a sullen expression exhibits loneliness and desolation.

But why are some expressions easily understood regardless of the differences in culture? How come body language breaks cultural communication barriers?

We have difficulty studying the evolution of language because the evidence is so sparse, and it does not leave any fossils. Only the uncovered skulls of Homo sapiens told our geologists and sociologists the overall shape and sizes of a hominid brain but not what it can do. All that was left in addition to the skull was the shape of the early man's vocal tract consisting of tongue, mouth, and throat.

It was not until the emergence of the modern humans that there were changes in the vocal tract that may have caused speech to be faster and more expressive. Some research even suggested that language began as a sign language before it gradually switched to the vocal modality.

How to Read Body Language

There are two sides to reading body language: Decoding and encoding.

Encoding is the ability to send or relay cues to others. This is the first impression that you give to other people and it is how you make them feel with you around.

Decoding is the ability to send cues to other people. It is how you read and interpret emotion, personality, and information people are trying to hide.

It's obvious that we humans are the only creatures that use words as communication. Animals, on the other hand, use nonverbal language and distinct sounds to communicate.

Whatever you do or whenever you speak, your body releases signals unknowingly. Those signals are read by others that see your body language. Most people believe it to be more reliable and more sincere than your very words. Your gestures speak a lot about your personality so that onlookers will tend to think of it as more accurate and true than what you actually say. So, it is really important that your words and actions synchronize so that you will not be at risk of delivering ambiguous messages and lose your credibility.

Do you remember a situation where you needed to use a service? People usually tell you all the things that you want to hear. They look sincere and friendly but there's something inside you that tells you not to trust them or that you don't like them; you are not at ease with them.

It could be because they haven't established a good rapport with you and without rapport, it will be difficult to work or be at ease with them. On the contrary, it could also be because their actions are incongruent with what they say or you've caught accidentally a body signal that they actually didn't mean to release. You call it most of the time a hunch or a gut reaction.

Because of these circumstances, you need to be aware of your body language signals to be an influencer and a better communicator. Then you can learn how to listen and understand other people's nonverbal language so that you can be a better communicator and have the ability to establish rapport. Anyway, every person has the natural ability to read body language for fifteen minutes and you can enhance it by teaching yourself and through practice.

Here are some points to consider when developing the skill:

Congruence

Be sure that your body language synchronizes with your words so that you won't give unintended messages.

Clear Mind

Concentrate on your goal or output. Your mind must understand clearly what you want to communicate and what your expected output is. It will not only motivate you but it will also bring out the natural genuineness in your words and gestures. Otherwise, if there is something that you don't understand clearly, it will surely reflect in your body signals even though it may not show in your words.

Believe Yourself

How could you make others believe in what you say if you don't believe it yourself? The tip here is that you believe your own words so that your body will correctly convey the message. According to the behavior cycle model, what you believe creates and affects your behavior (this includes your body language). Even if you don't believe what you are saying, tell it to yourself a couple of times so that you believe in it. Later, your body language will follow and synchronize with your words.

Avoid Exaggerations

Whenever you exaggerate by stressing out points, the more your body signals will betray you. So, if you are trying to be convincing, be brief and straight to the point.

Relax

When your muscles are tense, there is pressure building up inside. That means, natural looking body language is at risk. Just relax, take a deep breath and exhale. Your body will relax and your shoulders will drop. You can also shake your hands and feet a little to ease the tension. Just be sure that nobody sees you.

No Statues and Poker Faces

People will most likely be curious about why you are expressionless or remain as stiff as a statue. Using the poker-face technique is not a good option since it will make people wonder what you are hiding when you do so. It is good that you are conscious of what message your body will emit and when you try to control it. But move a little and act naturally. This will make people believe that you are sincere in what you say and do.

No Over-the-Top Hand Gestures

Hand gestures above the shoulders or high hand gestures will make you look awkward and less incongruent with what you are saying. This will also make you look that you are trying too hard. Just make your hand gestures between your waist and shoulders.

Avoid Fiddling and Comforting Habits

You may not be aware that you have pet fiddles. These are small, conscious or unconscious gestures that you do when you are anxious or you feel unsure. To determine if you have pet fiddles, ask a friend to observe your gestures for a while and tell you his or her observations. You can also do it yourself by recording your usual routines on a daily basis. You may discover that you fiddle with your hair, tie, jewelry, or your eyeglasses (if you wear them). If you have pet fiddles, train yourself to refrain from doing them. But if you still feel uncomfortable without fiddling, divert to something less noticeable like rubbing gently on the insides of your palm or thumb.

Trust and Honesty

If you are honest with what you say, you will have no problem with your body language. It will just be natural for you to be congruent with what you are saying especially when you trust others with what you are thinking and feeling instead of holding back. The best way to communicate is being true to yourself and avoid being sensitive and judgmental.

Feedback Mechanism and Reading Others

Gestures can have various interpretations just as a word can have a lot of definitions. But to be accurate in reading nonverbal intent, you have to consider the accompanying clues that go along with it.

Here are some basic tips:

- Arms that are crossed mean the person is either angry or anxious. It may also mean that he or she feels cold.
- Folded arms signals displeasure and the person wants to cut off what the other is saying. It could also indicate the other person feels comfortable doing it.
- Nose touching means that the person wants to cover up a lie but it can also simply mean that the nose is itchy.

Closed and Open Non-Verbal Communication

Observe a person's gestures when you negotiate with them and determine whether they have open or closed body language.

A closed body gesture means that the person you are negotiating with has a form of discomfort such as nervousness, fear, anxiety or hostility. This form of body language consists of gestures and posture that draw the body of the person in and towards the body itself. When the limbs are tense and closed in, the body appears smaller. When there is not much eye contact and the arms are folded, it often creates a barrier between the one who performs the action and the other person who sees it.

Open body language includes gestures or positions that indicate comfort, attentiveness, and relaxation. It welcomes the other person though it may also mean to others that you make yourself vulnerable to them. Otherwise, you show them that you are comfortable with them. When you exhibit open body language, your hands are in view and your palms are exposed. Good eye contact is present, and you are free and easy with your legs and posture.

Calibration

Sizing up a person's body language is a good tactic. Try to ask questions that you are guaranteed truthful answers—questions that have obvious answers—and pay attention. Do this at least three times to form a steady baseline.

If you notice changes in the baseline during the conversation, something is not right.

Practice being aware of other people's body language and try to decipher their gestures and posture by paying attention and staying in tune to what they are doing—it speaks so much about the person.

Most of the time, people tend to focus on their own thinking or what they are trying to say instead of noticing the other person's nonverbal communication. They even tend to forget or ignore what others are actually saying. If you try to observe other's actions consciously or unconsciously, you can become a better communicator.

Use It to Establish Rapport

When you speak with other people face to face, do you avoid looking at them most of the time? As for the others, when they speak, do you notice that they look away, too. Whenever you choose to look away, you are trying to remember vividly the situation by visualizing the moment, reliving your emotions or maybe you are searching for the right words that will fit into your story.

Establish rapport whenever you listen attentively and at the same time, you can also enhance your skills in reading body language. Just like when we talk on the phone, we make sounds that will ensure the other person that we are speaking to is still listening. It's also the same when we listen to the person who is talking to us (in face to face dialogue) although we don't make sounds.

Those who are experienced in communicating with other people slightly lean forward to the speaker as they make eye contact. These gestures assure the other person that they have their full attention, that they are listening, and they are keen on hearing more from the speaker. But listeners do not continuously stare because it will convey that they are not genuinely interested in the speaker's message.

Feel Comfortable or Just Chill

Relax. When you make yourself comfortable with another person, that person will also feel at ease with you. So, if you want a natural and enjoyable conversation, just relax to allow communication to flow smoothly.

You must not overlook and interpret a person's intention just because you identified the meaning of a single body gesture. Remember that when other words are used to construct a sentence, a group of body gestures can accurately point out the real intention of the portrayer. Here's a sample situation:

When a person crosses their arms, it may mean that they only feel cold. But when it is accompanied with back leaning, a step, or stiffening up, it means the person disagrees with what you are saying.

So, be observant and gather clues first before you conclude.

Chapter 2: The Significance of Learning and Understanding Non-verbal Communication

Non-Verbal Communication helps people to:

Reinforce or Modify What Has Been Spoken

When a person vehemently denies something, he or she will not just say "no!" They will include vigorous head movements to show strong disagreement.

When you meet a friend and ask how he or she is, the automatic answer is "I'm fine" with an added shoulder shrug. You may also notice that the person feels uncomfortable and can't look straight at you.

Convey Information About Emotional State

The way you communicate—the tone of voice, facial expression, and body language can tell people how you feel even without you telling them. How often have you heard people say "Are you sick?" or "You don't look fine!"

We know people can tell your state of emotion by simply looking at you.

Define or Reinforce Relationships Between People

When observing couples, you may notice how their movements are reflective of each other—holding hands, smiling, gazing into each other's eyes, etc. All these gestures are reinforcing their relationships; creating a strong bond, connecting them further.

Provide Feedback to the Other Person

When listening intently, you focus your eyes on the speaker letting them know that they have your full attention. Hand gestures indicate whether you are comfortable with another person or if you want to say something. When you agree, it is often accompanied by the nodding of your head or a slight upward movement of your brows when you are in doubt.

Regulate Communication Flow

There are many nonverbal cues to signal if you want conversation or a discussion to go on. An emphatic nod can indicate that you are in complete agreement with the speaker and have nothing more to say. On the other hand, connecting with the speaker along with a slight nod of the head can also imply that you wish to say something else.

Factors Affecting Understanding of Body Language

Understanding body language means seeing more than what you can see in the physical sense.

A person with arms folded could mean many different things:

- Feeling defensive
- Acting superior

- Judging
- Feeling relaxed

Here are the five points that will help you understand and see body language and non-verbal communication in a more realistic way:

Cues

When you act, it's not a stand-alone thing. You act in response to the actions done by others. Their actions caused by other people are what we call "triggers" that stimulate inner responses in us. Hence, seeing someone perform a particular action should make you ask yourself what led you to interpret their body language.

Cues can, likewise, occur internally in the case of thoughts and concerns leading to changes in body position. You may also ask yourself this, "Given this body language, what is the person thinking or feeling?"

You must be on the lookout for changes in a person's body language such as movements in the hands or legs, which is a sign of discomfort.

Once you see changes, look to see if there are clues to what triggered such change. An example is when someone lied and is confronted with a revealing question. There is this tendency to look away or lose eye contact.

Salesmen, likewise, study a customer's facial expressions, personal space, cheerful tones, and positive responses. Understanding their customer's body language is a signal to move further to close the deal.

Clusters

While changes in body language can single an action such as the crossing of arms, they often appear as a series of movements like when a person leans back a little, folds their arms, raises their eyebrows, and purses their lips. All these actions could mean one thing - disagreement.

A cluster of changes in body language all indicate one common emotion being felt at the moment. There are times when this cluster involves contradicting movements like when a person smiles but doesn't look straight or rubs their nose to hide discomfort. This indicates lying.

Character

Another explanation would be the general character of an individual. A person who is an introvert may use concise gestures as opposed to an extrovert who may display frequent and exaggerated body movements.

If you have no knowledge of an individual's character, it could be easy to confuse these gestures with timidity and exhibitionism. In seeking ways to predict a person's actions, we often make misinterpretations because of limited body signals and thereby assess and filter what we see based on incorrect mental models. Moods, temperaments, and other short-term emotions can also cause changes in our body language making it more difficult to interpret. However, if you are able to determine an individual's current emotional state, then you can apply this information to gain a better understanding of their actions.

Context

Lastly, the final factor to keep in mind when reading body language is the larger context that has a great influence on how the individual thinks, feels, and acts.

Events that may affect an individual can have a great impact on body language like when a person suddenly shifts their gaze, turns direction, and feel uncomfortable. It could be possible that the person suddenly saw someone they want to avoid and wants to get away. If you aren't aware of the situation, you won't be able to tell sudden changes in body language.

Chapter 3: Principles of Body Language

Body language plays a major role when people perceive your personality. Take listening skills for instance. Listening skills are a body language that most professions such as public service in particular, requires good relationships with clients. If you are a good listener, people tend to feel more comfortable with you even when you offer business advice, help people maintain their personal relationships with others, or give simple advice when you counsel them for any kind of problem that they may have.

Having poor body language can be a huge disadvantage when building future business relationships. Your nonverbal language tells people if you are genuinely interested in them and will determine your relationship. Therefore, it is very important to listen attentively to every word that's spoken and show sincere interest in regard to concerns.

The list below displays habits to avoid when listening:

- The habitual crossing of arms over your chest
- Impatient toe-tapping
- Leaning away
- Turning to look away often
- No eye contact or looking everywhere while a person is speaking

If you have any of these habits, people will think that you are not interested in what they're saying and may end your business relationship.

Try the steps below to improve your overall body language:

- Look at the person squarely in the face.
- To send a positive signal, avoid looking away.
- During communication, display an open pose. Never fold your arms or legs because the person that you are talking to will

think that you are not interested in listening.
- Lean forward while you are talking to someone. This means that you are paying attention.
- Maintain normal eye contact because it is crucial. Otherwise, it will show that you're not interested or comfortable.
- Maintain a relaxed posture – not too stiff or formal when you talk. Feel comfortable.

People aren't aware of how their body language speaks and communicates to others most of the time especially when they have no knowledge of its existence and importance.

Did you know that your body speaks to you all the time? You may not be conscious about it, but the moment you meet another person, your body communicates with them. Your body communicates through your hand gestures, stance, and the way you sit, even if words do not come out of your mouth. That is how other people perceive your way of communication.

But if your body language contradicts your intentions? Unfortunately, if that happens, onlookers will get the wrong message and it could damage your credibility. To prevent this from happening, you must have a clear understanding of body language.

You can maintain credibility by making a positive entrance positive every time you meet a business client. How? Talk about business as soon as you enter the room. This will ensure you are really interested, and you mean business. Searching for your briefcase and shuffling through paper will make a negative impression. If you have to wait for your customer, read a magazine.

Basic Tips on Body Language

Use the following tips to make a positive impression:

- Provide a warm and firm hand shake.

- Choose the most accessible seat and sit immediately.
- Do not give your customer the impression that you will sit only when you are asked to do so.
- Be mindful of the space between you and the customer. Never sit too far or too close.

Choose a seat according to your client's personality. If you think your client is a shy type, sit further away. The ideal distance between you and your client is between 20-50 inches. If you want to stress a certain point, lean forward to get closer.

Eye contact is essential, and it says a lot about your personality that should never go unnoticed.

If you want people to get the impression that you are honest, sincere and open, good eye contact plus a smile will do the trick. Poor eye contact and uneasy eyes (eyes that look in all directions repeatedly) mean that you lack self-confidence.

Constantly staring at the another person will also make them feel uncomfortable.

Your voice also plays an important role. Your tone is actually more important than the very words that you speak. Here, your body language is the tone of your voice so try to speak in your usual tone. When you use a normal tone and normal volume range, your body language is in an excellent state. If you want to exhibit professionalism, a well-modulated voice with a normal rate and rhythm shows passion and interest. If you want to grab your listener's attention, speak passionately. On the contrary, if you needlessly clear your throat or use 'ah' or 'um', this may mean that you are feeling anxious. Also, avoid using complicated sentences.

Focus on your gestures and posture to develop your body language. The following are simple tips to improve your posture and gestures:

Walk in an open manner- your posture should be erect when you stand; take easy and determined steps while your arms are swinging.

Demonstrate genuine listening- touch the bridge of your nose with your hand, cup your chin in between your index finger and thumb as you keep eye contact.

If you want to avoid negative impressions, try to avoid bad body language. Nervous movements can indicate disinterest. Be conscious of the body language that you transmit and avoid looking anxious. The following list includes common negative habits:

These habits mean that you disagree with another person's point of view:

- Crossing your legs
- Folding your arms over your chest
- Trying to pick up imaginary lint from your clothes

- Moving your hands on and around your face

These habits indicate a negative attitude:

- Coughing several times
- Blinking repeatedly
- Looking far away while the other person is speaking
- Shifting the eyes quickly and looking in different directions

The following may indicate frustration:

- Pointing your index finger at something
- Playing with your hair
- Wringing your hands
- Firmly clenching your hands

The following may indicate boredom:

- You don't focus your eyes on the speaker or no eye contact
- You sit with sloppy body posture

- You are preoccupied on something other than the person who is speaking

However, the importance of body language is more significant when you encounter people of diverse cultures.

Understanding body language is essential but you also need to take heed of other cues like context. Generally, it helps to see these signals as a group rather than just paying attention to a single action. When you are trying to read or interpret body language, here are the things you must watch out for:

How to Read People's Body Language

There are many ways we can convey emotions or messages through facial expressions. At times, you may express love, pity, anger, sadness, etc. to your partner through facial expressions. On the other hand, your partner must try to guess what emotion you are trying to convey. If you are good at reading emotions, then you can easily guess as long as your partner is good at conveying the emotion he or she was asked to project.

Generally, while you say you are fine when you're not, your facial expressions can display what you truly feel at the moment. Facial expressions reveal what you are trying to hide without you being aware of it. You may try to fake a smile, but you can't hide the pain in your eyes when you are hurt emotionally.

Here some examples of emotions that can be apparent in your facial expressions:

- Anger
- Surprise
- Disgust
- Hatred
- Fear
- Anxiety
- Confusion
- Excitement
- Desire
- Contempt

Disbelief and doubt can also be detected via facial expressions. A study revealed that a trustworthy person slightly raises their eyebrows along with a slight smile that conveys confidence and friendliness.

Among the various forms of body language, facial expressions are among the most universal. Expressions conveying fear, loneliness, anger, and happiness are the same.

Paul Ekman, a researcher, disclosed that we make judgments about people's intelligence based on what's shown across their faces. One study indicated that people with narrower faces and prominent noses are perceived to be intelligent. Those with cheerful expressions are bound to be more intelligent than those with angry faces.

The Eyes

Often times we've heard other people referring to our eyes as the window to the soul. Maybe it's because our lips can easily tell a lie but not our eyes. Notice that when you're guilty of something, you just can't look straight into another person's face. It's because your eyes are so sensitive that they can easily convey your inner feelings.

When you are engaged in a conversation with another individual, looking to their eyes is natural and significant to the process of communication. If you take note of the eye movement, you can see if the person you are talking to is:

- Averting their gaze
- Making direct eye contact
- Blinking their eyes

People may also have dilated pupils.

Pay Attention to the following signals:

Eye Gaze

A person who looks directly into your eyes while talking to you shows interest and is paying attention. However, prolonged eye contact can be disturbing and threatening. Breaking eye contact or trying to avert your gaze away from the person you are talking to can indicate that you are distracted or uncomfortable or it could be that you are concealing certain emotions.

Blinking

It's natural to blink your eyes once in a while but not too little or too much. People who are distressed or uncomfortable often blink their eyes but those who blink less frequently try to control their blinking to contain excitement. Poker players often use this technique so they can appear to be disinterested to their opponents.

Size of the Pupil

This can be a very subtle form of nonverbal communication. Though the level of lighting controls pupil dilation, there are times when emotion can cause a small change in the eye.

Have you ever heard the term "bedroom eyes?" People use this expression to indicate a desirous or sexually aroused look. On its lighter side, it is the kind of look that a man or women uses when they are interested in someone.

The Mouth

Another physical aspect that is significant in reading body language is the mouth. Habits like chewing on the bottom lip can show that the person is worried, insecure, fearful or anxious. Even smiles can be interpreted in many ways. A person can have a genuine smile or smile to cover up a feeling. Smiles can also be a sign of cynicism.

When you cough or yawn, your hand automatically covers up your mouth. Nonetheless, there are people who do this as an attempt to cover any facial expression showing disapproval.

When trying to assess a person's body language, pay attention to the following lip and mouth signals:

- Pursed lips
- The tightening of the lips means distrust, dislike, and disapproval
- Biting the lips indicates being stressed, worried, or anxious
- A mouth that is either turned up or down can indicate what a person is feeling at the moment. If the mouth is vaguely turned up, it is an indication of happiness. However, when the mouth is slightly turned downward, it means that a person is sad. This can also be a sign of disapproval or an outright grimace.

This is the clearest and obvious of all body signals. It is common to see someone waving, pointing or raising a hand to get someone's attention. Using hands to indicate numbers is also widely used all over the world and it is easily recognized by people in the different regions, states, or countries.

There are some cultural signs that are considered a positive sign in one region but abominable to others. An example of this is the circling of the thumb and index finger as a sign of money. It is not appropriate to use this hand signal when you are in Japan or in the Middle East countries as they consider it an abominable behavior.

Here are some common examples of hand signals and their meanings.

- The "OK" gesture is indicated by having your index finger and thumb touch each other forming a circle while the remaining fingers are extended. This means that you're okay. However, in some places in Europe, this can mean that you're nothing and the same signal is, likewise, considered vulgar in some parts of South America.

- A clenched fist can be a sign of anger or it can mean solidarity to some.
- The "V" sign that is made by lifting your index finger and middle finger and separating them to create a V-shape can either mean peace or victory in some countries. However, when the hand is facing outward, it can be offensive to Australians.

Arms and Legs

- Defensiveness can be shown by crossing the arms while crossing legs away from another person may show discomfort or dislike.
- Standing with hands on your hips is a sign of readiness and being in control though it can, likewise, be a sign off aggressiveness or being boastful.
- Clasping your hands behind your back indicates that you are bored, angry, or anxious.

- Restless tapping of fingers or fidgeting can signal that a person is frustrated, impatient or bored.
- Crossed legs mean that you are feeling closed off or in need of a little privacy.

How we sit, stand or hold our bodies can also tell a lot about us. Posture is our overall physical form and how we hold it. By merely looking at one's posture, you can determine a lot of information about how the person is feeling, their personality and characteristics - e.g., if the person is confident, shy, open or submissive.

- Sitting with the body hunched forward indicates that a person is bored and indifferent to their surroundings.
- When trying to read signals coming from an individual's posture, take note of the following:
    - When a person is sitting up straight, it means that they are a serious individual, focused, and

paying attention to what's going on around them.

- An open posture or the kind that keeps the trunk of the body open and exposed indicates openness, friendliness, and willingness. Closed posture, on the other hand, is where the trunk of the body is hidden because it is hunched forward hunching with the arms and legs crossed. This indicates unfriendliness, hostility, and anxiety.

Do you feel uncomfortable when someone comes too close to you?

There are people who don't want their personal space invaded by others. When someone comes too close for comfort, they feel uncomfortable.

Edward T. Hall, an anthropologist coined the term *proxemics,* which refers to the distance between people while in an interaction. Just when facial expressions and gestures tell much about a person, so does the physical space between two individuals.

Hall described the four levels of social distance that occur in different situations:

Intimate Distance (6-8 Inches Apart)

This distance indicates a closer relation or intimacy between two people where there is greater comfort involved. This can occur when two people are in an intimate position like hugging, kissing whispering, and touching.

Personal Distance (1.5 - 4 Feet Apart)

This indicates the level of distance between family members and close friends. The closer the distance that two individuals can interact comfortably indicates the level of intimacy in their relationship.

Social Distance (4-12 Feet Apart)

This is applicable to the distance between acquaintances. For someone you know fairly well like coworkers, you may be more comfortable interacting at a closer distance but for those you seldom see, a bigger distance can be more acceptable.

Public Distance (12-25 Feet Apart)

This range of physical distance is commonly used in public speaking. Talking to a large audience or giving a presentation at work is an example of this.

The level of distance that affects an individual's sense of comfort can vary with culture. This is the reason why we can experience culture shock from time to time when we travel abroad or even in another town far from where we live. Those living in Latin countries would find it more comfortable to get closer to one another while interacting but North Americans need more personal distance.

Chapter 5: The Language Differences in Sexes

Ever wondered if males and females have the same body language? To answer this, let's study their language cues.

Men are not as good as women in reading body language although they use different parts of their brains in doing so. According to Monica Moore from Webster University in St. Louis, men often miss a woman's first courtship signal. Usually, it takes a woman to eye-gaze three times before a man noticed her.

Moreover, women are better at reading body language because more of their brain cells are active every time they evaluate other behaviors. MRIs, likewise, revealed women have 14-16 active areas in the brain while studying other people's behavior while men only have 4-6.

When it comes to lying, men are motivated differently from women. While men lie to appear more successful, interesting, and powerful, women lie to protect others. They also lie about themselves. Men lie eight more times about themselves than women do.

Men's Body Language

If you know what you're looking for, the body language of a man is easier to read. Men have a certain way of standing, eye gazing, gesturing or shaking with their hands that will give you an idea about their real emotions and character.

Most often men think that they can fool people around them by showing them the behavior they are exhibiting. However, most of the time, they don't realize that their body language definitely exudes subtle signals for other people to see. Most of men's body language is hidden from them. So, if a person is trying to appear confident, their body language may show the opposite.

Studies on men's body language vary but have one point in common, which is the fact that body language makes up 50 - 80 of our communications. They also agree that there is body language that is common across all cultures.

Now, let's focus on the body language of men in particular. Studies show that conversation for men is largely a reflexive movement that does require much thought. However, some men have successfully learned to use body language and consciously use it to project the behaviors they want to convey to others.

Dominance

Men learn to project a dominant stance by standing with their shoulders squared off and hips facing forward with hands down at the sides. This shows that the man is extremely confident and, therefore, feels more dominant over another person. This stance can be used with intent when a man wants to exert dominance over someone.

Aggressiveness

With legs closed together and weight pushed forward, a man can have an aggressive stance. This can include shifting the dominant foot forward by about half a step. The head and chin might be slightly tilted forward or off-center.

Once the man takes this stance, it indicates that he is ready to fight - verbally or physically.

Being Defensive

When a man feels threatened, worried or fearful, he can easily move to the defensive stance. Here are a series of movements usually associated with the defensive stance:

- Feet turned outward
- Arms held close to the body
- Shoulders hunched
- Hands clasped in front
- Arms crossed over the chest or stomach

A man may resort to a defensive stance when they are feeling that they will be verbal or physical attacked by the person they are talking to.

Open Palms or Hiding the Palm

An open palm in men is a sign of openness, trust, and sincerity. It's like saying, I truly mean what I say. Having an open palm is a way of showing people that you are not holding any weapon that can harm anyone – literally or figuratively. This form of body language is often used by politicians.

Conversely, closing the hands into a fist conveys aggressiveness or being in a defensive position. If the palm of your hand is hidden like in a closed fist, you are trying to show dominance over another person or you could be defending someone.

Touching the Face

When men touch their face while talking, it is a sign of dishonesty or anxiety. Most gamblers use a poker face, but they can't help touching their faces when bluffing. Even politicians do this when being dishonest. Some job applicants touch their faces during interviews.

Fidgeting

Fidgeting is another form of body language that differs in men and women. When men fidget, it implies boredom but when women fidget while talking, it means they are anxious about something.

Handshake

A handshake is merely a form of greeting. However, there's much that can be revealed via your handshake. The strength applied during a handshake is just as important as when you offer to shake someone's hand. Many men are concerned with the strength of their grip but if you happen to grip too hard, it could mean that you are trying to impress the other party.

Dominant Handshake

A dominant man is easily detected through a handshake. When he tries to shake your hand and their palm facing downward, it indicates that the person is trying to establish dominance over the other person and is forcing them to meet their hand. The grip is firm but not tight and done with a forward lunge. Once the grip is tightened, it can be read as aggressiveness.

Submissive Handshake

If you palm is facing upward when shaking hands, it indicates submissiveness. The one offering an upturned palm may be intimated by the person they are shaking hands with or may feel inferior because the other person is an authority figure. If you don't want to feel intimidated, make sure to use a firm grip.

Two-handed Shakes

In a two-handed shake, if the hand opposite to the one being offered in a handshake comes up to grip the shaking hand, it indicates familiarity. This shows that you are very familiar with the other person and feel equally comfortable. This handshake is usually used between two individuals who are close to each other.

Eye Language

It is often said that eyes are the windows to the soul. While you are able to control the direction of your eyes, you can't control involuntary eye movement directed by your subconscious. These eye movements show what you're thinking and feeling.

Blinking

Random blinking of the eyes is normal. However, when blinking becomes rapid, it is a sign of stress. This abnormal type of blinking may indicate that a person is worried, agitated or feeling nervous. On the other hand, blinking that is slow and deliberate can be a sign of boredom or fatigue. It can be very hard to control eye movement such as blinking and is, therefore, a good indication of a person's current mood.

Focused Gaze

When naturally focusing your gaze, particularly on the lower half of the face, is an indication that you are paying attention to what is being said. On the other hand, a focused gaze with no eye movement, where the gaze is forced, is likely to indicate that someone is pretending to pay attention but is uninterested or thinking of something else.

Wider Gaze

A wider gaze that scans the whole face using natural eye movements indicates attention to the speaker. It can also mean that someone attracted to the person who is talking.

Upper Gaze

When someone focuses their gaze on the top of the head or just above the eyes of the person they are talking to, the gazer is trying to establish dominance. Woman interpret some gazes used by men as being sexist. If this happens to you, use your hands to redirect attention. However, if the man is dominant, he will continue to look over you.

Female Body Language

The body language of women does not completely vary from that of men. Nevertheless, female body language bears some remarkable contrast that makes it easily identifiable to women.

Women exhibit different courtship behavior compared to men, particularly if they're trying to entice the person they are attracted to. Here are some samples of their notable behavior:

- **Raising of Eyebrows**

    When women are trying to attract men, they unconsciously or consciously raise their eyebrows and lower their lids at the same time. This mimics their expression when they're experiencing pleasure.

- **The "Come-Hither" Look**

  The come-hither look is classic. The flirtatious glance is a woman's way to express her sexual intentions in a euphemistic manner.

- **The Sideway Glance**

  The sideways glance over raised shoulders features the soft curves of a woman's face. This denotes the presence of estrogen, which signifies fertility. The gesture also releases pheromones, a hormone responsible for sexual arousal. Women instinctively glance sideways when they're trying to flirt.

- **Hair Flipping**

  Women naturally toss (or flip) their hair or touch their neck when flirting. This gesture reveals the armpit and releases pheromones, highlights their crowning glory, and exposes the curvature of their neck. These factors help deepen the attraction of the opposite party.

Women sometimes find it hard to show their confidence sans intimidation. They use body cues to show vulnerability (or submissiveness) and use subtle hints of assertiveness at the same time in order to convey the silent message that their femininity does not equate to meekness.

Women usually raise their eyebrows higher to show helplessness. As a natural reaction, a man's brain secretes a hormone connected with defending or protecting the female.

When women feel confident, they stand with their feet apart. At times, they toss their hair and lift their chins up with a playful smile in their lips.

Smile

Most people assume that a smile portrays happiness. Rarely does one think that it's a sign of nervousness. Women usually hide their nervousness with a smile. You will notice this when she excessively does this even at inappropriate times.

Leaning Forward

Women lean forward when they engage in an earnest conversation. They also do this when they're flirting with somebody they like. It is important for you to take note of the key cues to accurately interpret the meaning of this particular body language.

Eye Rolling

Women usually roll their eyes out of frustration or impatience although they sometimes use this as a pretend sarcasm. When a woman stays verbally quiet and reserved but rolls her eyes, it means that she's trying to stay polite but is already losing her patience.

Eye Contact

Direct eye contact is often encouraged in Western culture. It conveys positive messages such as paying attention to the conversation and a sign of attraction. People who have a steady gaze are often perceived to be trustworthy but those who have a hard time maintaining eye contact might be a disinterested or submissive (or much worse—a liar).

However, direct eye contact is not encouraged in the East Asian culture wherein the lack of direct eye contact means reverence. Japanese women avoid looking at men to show their respect and not because she's shy or doesn't have self-confidence. Again, you have to exercise proper discretion for this particular body language.

Dilated Eyes

A woman's eyes dilate when they see something they want or like. If you've asked the woman you like for a date and her eyes dilate, you have a big chance to hear a positive reply. If you present a woman with an option she likes, you will also get this reaction.

Rapid Blinking of Eyes

Aside from circumstances when a woman is obviously flirting, rapid blinking of her eyes might mean that she's uncomfortable or nervous. If you approach a woman and she's blinking rather excessively (and not even smiling), then she's anxious or scared.

Lip Gestures

Many men think that when a woman bites her lower lip, she's seducing them. Women also do this gesture when worried, anxious or stressed out. When a woman intends to seduce a man, she will bite her lip along with an intense gaze.

When a woman tightens her lips while listening to someone, she's expressing silent but strong disapproval. She's having a hard time holding her emotions and is fighting whatever negative retort she's thinking. When women do this, it means that they intensely dislike or resent another person.

Handshake

A weak handshake indicates that a woman is nervous, shy, submissive, intimidated or a combination of all of these. On the flip side, a woman with a strong handshake means that she's confident and in control.

Hands on Hips

When men see a woman putting her hands on her hips during a conversation, it means that she's getting aggressive. By putting the hands on the hips (and sometimes with feet apart to take a wider stance), a woman unconsciously tries to get bigger; thus, looking more intimidating in the process. When the hands are clenched tight, it portrays a higher degree of hostility. A woman may be extremely difficult to placate when this occurs. If this happens, it's best to do something to break the aggression.

Exposed Wrist or Open Palm

The wrist is a vulnerable part of a woman's body just like the neck. When displayed, it signals submission. Many women unconsciously show an open palm or exposed wrist whenever they're ready to obey. She is more likely to listen to your requests or bow to your authority.

Expressive Hand Gestures

A lot of women use excessive hand gestures whenever they're completely absorbed and emotionally involved in the topic of their conversation. It's important to understand that expressive hand gestures specifically those at or above the shoulders depicts lack of emotional control. If you want to be taken seriously, limit your hand gestures or maintain them below the waist.

Locked Ankles

A woman who locks her ankles while standing or sitting might feel distressed, nervous or guilty.

However, this is not true at all times as the gesture might be due to the way a woman is dressed. Women who wear miniskirts tend to cross their ankles for apparent reasons. Reserved women also have a habit of locking their ankles whenever they sit.

Chapter 6: Benefits of Knowing How to Read Body Language and Facial Expressions

Experts reveal that nonverbal cues a substantial portion of our communication. These unspoken cues actually "speak" louder than spoken words. The slightest movement of our brows or our unconscious fidgeting reveals our concealed emotions. In courtroom settings, lawyers can use nonverbal hints in order to sway the opinions of jurors. For example, the attorney may glance at his watch to convey that the opposing lawyer's argument is getting tedious. These nonverbal signals work so effectively and powerfully that some judges put limits on what types of nonverbal behavior one must observe during courtroom sessions. Let's talk more about the advantages of knowing how to read nonverbal signals.

Enhance Parenting Skills

Children are more perceptive than we think. Your body language and facial expressions can be effective when communicating with your children. You might not be aware that you're sending negative messages to your kids even without speaking them out loud. Improving your nonverbal skills can effectively boost your parenting skills in the process. Below are some examples of how you can use nonverbal communication to improve your parenting skills:

- A hug can effectively reassure a crying baby or child that everything's going to be all right.
- Taking time to listen and establishing eye contact as your child tells an important story, adventure, and school experience. Avoid multitasking because your child will think that you are not interested.
- A pat on the back (or head) or high-five shows that you're proud of your child.

- A handshake given to your teenage child means that you recognize their maturity, growth, and achievement.

Give Good Impression in Job Interviews

Observing proper nonverbal communication can be as powerful as providing the right verbal answers during a job interview. On the flip side, poor nonverbal cues might hinder an interviewee's success in the interview since they tell a lot of things about you. Arriving late for your interview symbolizes that you're an irresponsible, inefficient or simply not interested in the position you're applying for. On the contrary, being ton time conveys a positive message. Another nonverbal form of communication that you need to establish in order to make a good impression is your handshake. It should be firm and strong, lasting between three to four seconds. Make eye contact with the interviewer as you shake hands with a complete grip.

Nourish Personal Relationships

As established, nonverbal cues help you communicate various emotions to the people around you, particularly to your family. This is why unspoken rules are sometimes established. You begin to understand each other in a deeper sense. For example, one sharp look from a mother signifies that something shouldn't be done. A bubbly child's silence might mean that he or she is keeping a secret or that there might be a problem.

Identify and Read Negative Nonverbal Behavior

Having the ability to identify and understand nonverbal cues in other people will help you easily recognize negative emotions and unspoken issues.

Let's face it—we cannot avoid difficult conversations with people, whether with our family, friends, a boss, a colleague or a complete stranger. It's a painful fact of life everybody has to face at some point and time. However, it doesn't mean that you have to remain ignorant of ways on how to ease these difficult situations. You can stay composed in order to resolve the issues in a level-headed manner. But complicated feelings like anger, stress, anxiety, and defensiveness will still remain and can be reflected in our body language and facial expressions. The following behaviors show that a person is either unhappy or emotionally detached:

- The body is turned away from you
- Arms folded in front of the body
- Tense facial expression
- Downcast eyes, looking away or maintaining little eye contact

Recognizing these signs can help you easily adjust your response and how to say it in a way that won't make the situation worse or help others see your perspective.

When you need to collaborate with your team, deliver a presentation to the board or teach students, you want them to be completely engaged with you. Otherwise, you're simply wasting your time. Here are some examples that identify when your audience is bored or uninterested:

- Gazing into space or at something else
- Doodling or drawing
- Fidgeting
- Looking at phones or playing with pens
- Slouching with heads tilted down
- Picking at clothes

When you notice these signals, you can immediately do something to keep your audience engaged. For instance, you can attract their attention by asking questions or inviting them to state their own opinions or ideas.

Project Yourself Positively

Positive body language and facial expressions attract people and bring out your confidence. Below are a few tips to help you:

Observe a Positive Posture

Stand or sit straight (avoiding being stiff), with your shoulders back and arms at your sides or in front of you. Do not slouch, tilt your head downwards or put your hands inside of your pockets.

Practice Your Body Language

Look in the mirror and practice your posture. Avoid being stiff while sitting or standing. Evenly distribute your weight, keeping one foot slightly in front of the other as this will help maintain your posture.

Use Open Hand Gestures

Keep your upper arms close to your body as you spread your hands apart, palms slightly facing towards your audience. This stance shows your willingness to communicate and share ideas with your audience or the people around you. However, avoid exaggerating your gestures as people might get distracted by your movements instead of what you're actually saying.

Keep Your Head Up

Keep your head upright and level. Avoid leaning far back or forward since this makes you look arrogant or aggressive.

Have a Relaxed and Open Facial Expression

People will automatically see and feel your discomfort if you look stiff or frozen. Smile the way you would do with your friends—with warmth and sincerity. Remember, people are attracted to confident, warm, and genuine individuals.

Learning how to read and interpret these subtle hints will enable you to gain an advantage. For instance, it will help you fully comprehend the message of the person you are talking to and boost our understanding of people's reactions to what we say and do. Furthermore, you can modify your body language to appear more positive, agreeable, and appealing.

Facial Profiling

Facial profiling is identifying a person's personality by analyzing their facial features. It is a form of physiognomy, the concept that one's personality can be gauged through the analysis of his or her facial features. According to accumulated research in the field of social and life sciences, personalities are affected by our genes and our face is a reflection of our DNA. There are no clear, solid pieces of evidence that directly identify physiognomy as a reliable tool but recent studies have suggested that analysis on facial appearance contains a relevant amount of truth about a person's personality and character.

Reading faces can be a vital skill particularly when you meet and communicate with a lot of people on a daily basis. You will have the ability to take care of the people closest to you, have a better understanding of your co-workers and clients, and gauge the hidden emotions of the people you come in contact with.

So, how do you read and analyze facial features to determine the personality of a certain individual? For starters, you have to consider the following elements:

- Face shape, ears, and hair
- The shape and size of the lips, mouth, and chin
- Length and shape of the nose
- Color, size, shape, and distance between the eyes and eyebrows
- The type and size of the forehead including the wrinkles and their alignment

Face Shape

Oval

People with an oval-shaped face are sweet, charming, and have a balanced personality, which is why they're often the best pacifiers or diplomats. Women with oval faces in particular, are often the best artists. These people can also be phlegmatic and inactive.

Round

This is also known as a water-shaped face since the face is normally plump. These people are known to be empathetic and caring. They also have strong sexual fantasies. If you desire a long-term relationship, people with round faces can be a great choice.

Oblong

People with an oblong-shaped face have cheekbones not wider than their jawline and forehead. They are usually practical, organized, and are workaholics. They also have a strong inclination to narcissism and problematic relationships.

Rectangle

Rectangular-faced individuals can also be domineering but not as much if compared to their square-faced peers. They're also active in the field of sports, politics, and business. They are usually ambitious and melancholic.

Square

People with a square-shaped face are highly analytical and intelligent. They have decisive, aggressive, and dominating personalities.

Diamond

This face shape is characterized by prominent cheekbones, a pointed chin, and a regular nose. They are confident, perfectionists, and determined. These qualities make them good leaders. On the other hand, they can be unpredictable and quick-tempered. They usually have problematic relationships and achieve success late in life.

Triangle

People with triangular face have a wide forehead, straight cheekbones that taper from the jawline to the forehead, and a square and/or flat chin. They are active but have low stamina. They are highly intelligent, creative and vivacious although they easily get depressed, emotional, and sensitive.

Heart or Inverted Triangle

Heart-shaped faces are characterized by large foreheads and a V-shaped jawline. These people are great in self-analysis, quick-thinking, and have a good memory. They also love independence, sincerity, and commitment. They are very ambitious by nature.

Hair

Black

People with straight black hair are usually calm, melancholic, and pessimistic. On the other hand, curly-haired ones are genial, affectionate, and positive.

Blond

This hair color reflects obedience, naiveté, and freshness. Blond-haired people are often physically weak but have an excellent memory. They can be impressionable and indifferent at the same time.

Brown

Generally, people with brown hair are quite romantic but indifferent at times. They love to travel and experience adventures. They have strong character and radical ideas. Those with dark brown, silky hair can be seductive, sensible, proud, confident, and sociable. Those with coarse brown hair are independent, resilient, hardworking, reliable, and responsible. They are exemplary in handling finances.

Red

People with dark red hair are usually temperamental, skeptical, quarrelsome, and courageous. They are often endowed with great physical prowess. Bright red-haired individuals have sensitive, intelligent, and lustrous spirits. Those with silky hair have a loving and passionate nature. If red-haired people have fair skin, they often have a high artistic sense and are highly imaginative.

Hairy People

Men who have hairy bodies can be sentimental. They are also strong and energetic, leading them to excel in sports. On the contrary, those who have no hair can be cunning, clever, and dominating. They also have high business acumen.

Eyebrows

Straight

People with straight brows are direct, technical, and realistic. They appreciate logic and need to be presented with facts and relevant data in order to be thoroughly convinced. They can also separate their emotions so that their judgment won't be clouded.

Curved

This means that a person is people-oriented. People with curved eyebrows have the ability to relate and connect to the world through their understanding of people. They are quite pragmatic and learn best through personal experiences. They hate technical details and theories but prefer the practical approach instead.

Angled

People with angled eyebrows stay calm in any given situation. They are gregarious and have great leadership qualities. They are usually mentally focused and often do the right thing.

Low

Expressive and impulsive—that's how people with low eyebrows are. They can quickly assess and process information; hence, they also have the ability to make snap decisions. They are "doers" instead of "thinkers" and want to get the job done right away. Moreover, these people tend to be optimistic at first but become antagonistic when criticized. They lack patience and are always on-the-go.

High

High eyebrows denote discerning. These people take their time to observe and sort out their ideas before actually acting on a certain situation. They need thorough information in order to deeply understand a subject, a mystery, or a puzzle. They store information with an emotional mark so that when they recall the feeling or emotion, they can automatically remember the event or information with great clarity. They find it hard to make snap decisions or assessments as they always need time to reflect on matters.

Bushy

Bushy brows denote great intellectual capacity. These people never run out of ideas as they are mentally active.

Winged

Winged brows are characterized by a thick beginning and a thinner end. These people are great planners as they always come up with huge new ideas. They are visionaries, allowing them to create new challenges. However, they can be quite weak in follow-throughs.

Pencil-Thin

People with fine-lined brows are often associated with single-mindedness. They can only focus on a certain thing at a time. They also tend to be overly sensitive or self-conscious and can be people-pleasers.

Even

This brow type has the same thickness all throughout its length. People with even brows possess mental clarity. Ideas tend to flow smoothly and consistently, making it easier for these people to grasp whole concepts. They tend to be intolerant of "slow" people or those who can't instantly get their ideas.

Managerial

Managerial brows are characterized by a thin beginning and thicker outer edges. People who possess this brow type can do great follow-through. They are well-organized and methodical, making them the right people in roles that require meticulous attention and detailed work.

Access

Characterized by hairs growing straight at the beginning of the brows, these people have a deep and strong connection between their logical mind and inner emotions. They can instantly pinpoint potential problems. Those who only have excess hair on the right brow mean that they can spot dilemmas in the field of business. If it's on the left, they can predict or anticipate probable complications within a relationship.

Tangled or Wild

Wild brows indicate unconventional thinking. These people can see and assess the various facades of a certain issue. They have the ability to play the devil's advocate and unravel hidden truths and mysteries. Their unusual way of thinking also attracts unwanted trouble or conflict.

Chameleon or Nearly Invisible

These people are known to have the ability to easily blend into any group. They are great negotiators and can be great spies since they have the talent to extract information from certain people.

Eyes

Black

Black eyes convey mystery and secrets. People with black eyes are often secretive but trustworthy. They are also practical, optimistic, passionate, and charismatic. Most of them are also natural-born leaders.

Brown

Individuals with brown eyes are energetic, creative, courageous, persistent, and productive. They don't value material gains too much. Instead, they focus their attention on nature, spirituality, and freedom.

Hazel

This color is actually a mixture of green and brown. Hazel-eyed people are brave, independent, sensible, and spontaneous. If the brownish shade is more abundant, it means that the person is approachable.

Gray

Grey-eyed people are sensitive, have great analytical prowess, and possess a great deal of inner strength. They are also versatile as they can easily switch their moods to suit the present situation.

Blue

Blue eyes are considered to be most desirable as most people associate this eye color with eternal youth. People with light blue eyes have the tendency to be competitive, skeptical, and egocentric. On the other hand, those with darker shades are often more agreeable.

Green

According to a study, green eyes are often connected to sexiness and creativity. Green-eyed people also resort to underhanded tactics.

Monolid

People with single-fold eyelids tend to be logical, rational, and stubborn. They also have the ability to manage their finances wisely.

Double-Fold Eyelids

Those with double-fold eyelids are often emotional, sentimental, impulsive, bold, and eccentric. They can be flexible and talented when it comes to acquiring financial resources. Unfortunately, they also have a weak sense of handling their finances.

Hooded Eyes

Hooded eyelids are depicted as being partially covered by skin that drops down from the brow bone, making one look sleepy. These people possess the characteristics that both monolid and double-folded eyelid people have. They have an implicit and temperate style and can be reserved. They work carefully but seem to lack in spirits so only a few of them tend to become leaders.

Other Attributes

People with large, round eyes are usually flirty and affectionate. They are intelligent, imaginative, and quite impulsive. If there's a big space between the eyes, it means that you prioritize honesty and simplicity. If their eyes are close together, they are focused but can also be restless.

Individuals with small eyes are observant, cunning, and malevolent. They are opportunity seekers and tend to take advantage even of the smallest things.

People with a closed set of eyes have the talent to quickly learn foreign languages. They also have a good memory.

Nose

Aquiline

Those with an aquiline nose have a commanding personality. They are proud and determined.

However, if the nose is too narrow, the person can be rather dictatorial.

Straight

People with a straight and proportioned nose tend to be patient, kind, elegant, and persevering. They have well-balanced personalities although they can also be cold and indifferent at times. They usually have liberal ideas in areas of moral and social aspects of life.

Meanwhile, those who have a straight nose with the nose tip bent downwards are usually melancholic and lenient.

Pointing Up and Slightly Curved In

These people are often enthusiastic and skillful. They can efficiently implement their strategies despite the obstacles. They are always cheerful, stylish, and optimistic about their goals. One can't be mad at them for too long due to their nature.

Snub

People with a snub nose often display dominance and lack of elegance in many aspects of life. However, they can be eloquent speakers and have literary and poetic prowess.

Curved

A curved nose exhibits sharpness, indifference, and hostility. Partnered with thin lips and bent mouth edges, it conveys that the person is gossipy.

Cheeks

Fleshy or Meaty

People with fleshy cheeks are usually artistically inclined and have a special sensitivity.

Round and Full

Those with round cheeks are innocent and languid.

Sunken

Sunken cheeks are often associated with people who are morose, depressed, and often sick.

Extra Smooth

Those who have very smooth cheeks are usually carefree.

Furrowed

People with furrowed cheeks are simple and unsophisticated. They are also happy workers but are not workaholics.

Raised to the Eye

These people are warm, generous, compassionate and sympathetic. Their ultimate weakness is being receptive since they lack critical ability.

Lips

Thick

Thick lips are often associated with a loving character. However, if it's coupled with a split chin, it means laziness and selfishness.

Thin and Small

Those who have these types of lips are often cold, calculating, and cruel.

Pale and Tight

Accompanied by square jaws, this person is greedy, cruel, brutal, and selfish personality.

Upper Lip Partly Covers the Lower Lip

People who have this lip type are usually good-natured, loving, and favor entertainment. If the lips are thin, it signifies parsimony and selfishness.

Heart-Shaped

It conveys independence and confidence. People who have heart-shaped lips are sensual and seductive by nature.

Pronounced Lower Lip

These people can be sarcastic and highly satirical but have exemplary intelligence.

Ears

Small ears display affection, honor, and impeccable manners. If the earlobe is thick, this person is rather emotional. If the ears are too small, the person is reserved and shy. Medium ears show determination and energy.

Big ears with thick earlobes often indicate the person is materialistic and rude by nature. Distanced ears show cruelty and destructive desires.

You can determine if your ears have a normal height when they don't pass above the level of the eyebrows and are nose level. People Those with ears to past the height of the eyebrows are usually angry, vengeful, and have criminal tendencies.

People with detached earlobes are generous and free-spirited. Those with attached earlobes can be stingy and observe strict self-discipline. A large distance between the eyes and ears presents great talent and intelligence.

Forehead

A high forehead shows diligence, discipline, and success in the future. These people are scholarly.

People with a low and wide forehead are very intuitive, imaginative, and extremely talented. They love spontaneity and freedom. Their interest centers on impressions more than the knowledge gained through studies.

Meanwhile, a high and slightly wide forehead partnered with well-shaped eyebrows is the most coveted since it denotes permanent success.

A square forehead means that the person prioritizes honesty and sincerity. If it is partnered with straight eyebrows, these qualities are intensified.

A forehead lined with deep wrinkles signifies that the person indulges in deep research and contemplation. Vertical wrinkles between the eyes show that the person deeply concentrates.

On the other hand, a forehead without wrinkles shows selfishness, sarcasm, and lack of empathy.

Chin

Those who have a protruding and round chin exhibit determination, prudence, wisdom, and strength. They encourage confidence through their easy and pleasant attitude.

Those who have a round dimpled chin have good business acumen.

People who have a long, square chin can be great in law enforcement and finances. However, if a person also has small tight lips, it means that they're relentless.

A bony and square chin show that they have strength of character and are slow to anger. Meanwhile, a dimply square chin shows a fiery temper and obstinate nature.

Double chin and fleshy cheeks reveal a personality that is fond of sensual pleasures and good food. These qualities are increased when a person also has large jaws.

Identifying Personality Types

Personality typing is the process of categorizing the personalities of different people according to the way they act or think. These personality types were created by Isabel Briggs Myers and Katharine Briggs in the 1960s and were based on the work of the renowned psychologist, Carl Jung. According to them, there are four key dimensions that can be utilized to classify personalities:

- Judging vs. Perceiving
- Introversion vs. Extraversion
- Sensing vs. Intuition
- Thinking vs. Feeling

Each of these four key dimensions was characterized as a *dichotomy* or a preference between two styles of being. The sum of a person's four preferred styles describes their personality type.

According to their theory, each of these dimensions were combined to generate predictable patterns in behavior and thought, so that people with the same four preferences share many attributes in how they approach their lives (e.g. common hobbies and suitable job or career).

Nothing among these personality types is considered "better" or "the best." The categorization process was mainly designed to help an individual know themselves better. It is not by any means to be taken as a tool to make someone look abnormal or dysfunctional.

Each personality type was given a letter code that stands for a preference in the manner of behaving and thinking.

Judging or Perceiving (J/P)

The dimension of Judging/Perceiving is characterized by how people deal with their lives.

Judgers prefer things to be planned and organized, considering the structure and order of the highest importance. They dislike last-minute change of plans.

Perceivers, on the other hand, value spontaneity and flexibility. They like things to be open in order to leave room for changes.

Introversion or Extraversion (I/E)

The dimension of Introversion/Extraversion depicts how an individual manages their energy.

Introverts are energized by spending time with a small group (usually family or closest friends) and feel recharged by spending time alone. They are reserved and contemplative.

Extraverts (or *extroverts*) tend to be action-oriented since they feel energized by other people or being busy. They are outspoken, expressive, and sociable.

Sensing or Intuition (S/N)

The Sensing/Intuition scale determines how a person gathers and processes information around them.

Sensors utilize their five senses and pay more attention to reality or the information they can clearly see, feel or touch, hear, smell, and taste. They are known as practical learners.

Intuitives focus more on the abstract level of thinking as they love to think about patterns, impressions, and theories. They have a creative streak and are often more apprehensive of the future than the present.

Thinking or Feeling (T/F)

The Thinking/Feeling scale focuses on how a person makes decisions based on the information accumulated by sensing or using intuition.

Thinkers place a greater emphasis on logic, facts, objective data, and sound reasoning. In short, they make decisions with their heads. They tend to be logical, consistent, and impersonal when contemplating their decisions.

Feelers prefer feelings, giving importance to their emotions so they usually decide with their hearts. Their values and principles greatly influence the decisions they make.

Each personality type is given a four-letter code which serves as an acronym for the four main dimensions of one's personality.

ISTJ (Introverted, Sensing, Thinking, Judging): The Inspector

People with ISTJ personality types love to organize and plan all the aspects of their lives particularly their family and work. They tend to be reserved, realistic, and loyal. They also place emphasis on laws and traditions, preferring to follow established rules and procedures.

Strengths

- Observant
- Realistic and Practical

- Logical
- Organized
- Detail-oriented
- Focused on the present

Weaknesses

- Subjective
- Judgmental
- Insensitive

Career Paths

Because of their nature, INTJ types tend to excel in jobs with clearly defined schedules, strong focus on tasks, and precise assignments. Popular jobs for this personality type include:

- Lawyer
- Accountant
- Detective
- Police officer
- Computer programmer
- Doctor
- Dentist

- Military leader
- Librarian

Famous People with INTJ Personalities

- Queen Elizabeth II
- Henry Ford
- US Pres. George Washington

ISTP (Introverted, Sensing, Thinking, Perceiving): The Crafter

Individuals with the ISTP personality type enjoy spending time alone whether they go on adventures, new experiences, work, or other activities. These people are passionately independent. ISTPs are also logical, rational, practical, and result-oriented. They prefer hands-on activities instead of musing on abstract ideas or concepts. They love doing new things and tend to quickly get bored with routine.

Strengths

- Practical learner
- Realistic and logical

- Easygoing and confident
- Cool-headed and composed
- A powerful focus on maintaining their objectivity
- Great in coping with crisis

Weaknesses

- Insensitive
- Dislikes commitment
- Thrill seekers and risk-takers
- Can easily get bored
- Difficult to read what they actually feel

Career Paths

Since ISTPs are introverted, they usually prefer to do jobs that don't necessarily require teamwork. They dislike structure but love freedom and autonomy. Since they're logical, they enjoy jobs that involve reasoning and practical experiences like:

- Forensics expert
- Engineer

- Software engineer
- Computer programmer
- Video game designer
- Law enforcer
- Scientist
- Pilot
- Firefighter

Famous People with ISTP Personalities

- Amelia Earhart
- US Pres. Zachary Taylor
- Clint Eastwood

ISFJ (Introverted, Sensing, Feeling, Judging): The Protector

ISFJ is one of the most common types of personality. People with ISFJ personalities are known to be warm-hearted and responsible. Since they are introverted, they can be quiet, reserved, and very observant. They are particularly in harmony with the emotions and feelings of the people around them.

Strengths

- Reliable
- Detail-oriented
- Perceptive
- Realists
- Practical

Weaknesses

- Neglects their own needs
- Often avoids confrontation
- Dislikes change (especially big ones)
- Disapproves abstract ideas and concepts

Career Paths

Since ISFJs stay in tune with the feelings of other people, they are effective in the healthcare industry or in jobs requiring attention to detail, planning, managing, and administering. They are highly organized, meticulous, independent, and reliable. Here are some of the ideal jobs for individuals with ISFJ personalities:

- Nurse

- Counselor
- Social worker
- Child care provider
- Bookkeeper
- Administrator
- Office manager
- Teacher
- Banker
- Accountant
- Paralegal

Famous People with ISFJ Personalities

- Prince Charles of Great Britain
- Louisa May Alcott
- Mother Teresa

ISFP (Introverted, Sensing, Feeling, Perceiving): The Artist

People with ISFP personalities are usually described as peace-loving, quiet, and easy-going. There are only five to ten percent of people with this type of personality.

While ISFPs can be reserved, that doesn't mean that they are cold. They're caring, peaceful, and considerate to others. Like the first three personality types, the "artists" dislike dwelling in abstract thinking and favor hands-on experiences.

Strengths

- Loyal to their beliefs, values, and principles
- Practical
- Mindful of their environment

Weaknesses

- Hates theoretical information and abstract ideas
- Intensely dislikes confrontations and arguments
- Strongly prefers to be alone

Career Paths

ISFP personalities have a strong appreciation of nature particularly animals. They go after hobbies or jobs that put them in contact with the great outdoors. Since they also love to focus on the present, they stand out in careers that exercise practicality and solve real-world problems. These jobs suit ISFPs best:

- Artist
- Designer
- Composer
- Musician
- Forest ranger
- Naturalist
- Pediatrician
- Psychologist
- Chef
- Teacher
- Veterinarian

Famous People with ISFP Personalities

- Marilyn Monroe

- David Beckham
- Auguste Rodin

INFJ (Introverted, Intuitive, Feeling, Judging): The Advocate

INFJ people are also known as the "Idealist" and are said to be one of the rarest personality types, consisting only of one to three percent of the population. They're known to be caring, gentle, and creative. Although they are often reserved, they are also highly responsive to the feelings of others. They rather enjoy thinking arcane topics and meditating about the meaning of life.

Strengths

- Idealistic
- Have strong intuition and emotional understanding
- Perceptive of the needs of other people
- Highly artistic and creative
- Future-focused
- Like abstract thinking

- Value close, deep relationships

Weaknesses

- Overly sensitive
- Stubborn
- Dislikes conflict and confrontation
- Difficult to understand at times

Career Paths

INFJs have a high artistic sense so they excel in jobs where they can express their creativity. However, their personality puts greater emphasis on deeply rooted values and convictions; thus, they can truly blossom in jobs that support these principles. They will do best in careers where they can integrate their creativity to generate significant changes in the world.

As INFJs excel in academics and their workplace, they can be perfectionists at times. They tend to be critical of themselves and strive harder in the process. Their colleagues also respect these qualities so it's only natural that they work well together. These job work best with this personality type:

- Actor
- Artist
- Writer
- Musician
- Photographer
- Counselor
- Psychologist
- Teacher
- Librarian
- Religious worker
- Entrepreneur

Famous People with INFJ Personalities

- Carl Jung
- Oprah Winfrey
- Martin Luther King, Jr.
- Taylor Swift

INFP (Introverted, Intuitive, Feeling, Perceiving): The Mediator

People with this personality type tend to be idealistic, introverted, creative, and motivated by moral values and principles. They have strong humanitarian interests and goals like making the world a better place. Moreover, they understand themselves better and know their life goals. These people search for their own purpose in life and how they can use their skills, knowledge, and talents to better serve others.

Strengths

- Devoted
- Perceptive
- Caring and have a genuine interest in others
- Puts emphasis on close relationships
- Has the ability to determine important facts and effects of a situation

Weaknesses

- Can be overly idealistic
- Difficult to understand at times
- Weak attention to details
- Has the tendency to take things personally

Career Paths

They normally do well in jobs where they can express their vision and creativity at the same time. While they can be great team players, they prefer working alone. They're passionate about defending and advocating their own set of beliefs. At the same time, they're interested in learning more about other beliefs and consider various facades of a certain issue. Below are the jobs suitable for INFPs:

- Physical Therapist
- Psychologist
- Counselor
- Social Worker
- Artist
- Writer
- Graphic Designer

- Librarian

Famous People with INFP Personalities

- William Shakespeare
- JRR Tolkien
- Audrey Hepburn

INTJ - The Architect

Also known as the "Strategist," INTJ people are highly analytical, creative, and logical. There are only one to four percent of people in the population that fall into this category.

Strengths

- Great listeners
- Love theoretical and abstract concepts
- Take criticism well
- Self-confident
- Hard-working

Weaknesses

- Perfectionist

- Tendency to be overly analytical and judgmental
- Insensitive
- Despises talk about feelings or emotions

Career Paths

INTJs are great at gathering information, analyzing it, and provide new insights. Since they value information, intelligence, and knowledge, they make exemplary scientists and mathematicians. They also excel as the following:

- Engineer
- Dentist
- Doctor
- Teacher
- Judge
- Lawyer

Famous People with INFP Personalities

- C.S. Lewis
- Hannibal
- Arnold Schwarzenegger

INTP (Introverted, Intuitive, Thinking, Perceiving): The Thinker

These people are quiet and analytical, favoring their time alone to delve deeper into abstract concepts and theories. They never get tired of their inner world but tend to marvel in it every single time. Although they have wide social circles, they prefer to be close to a selective few. Only one to five percent of the population has this personality type.

Strengths

- Objective and logical
- Loyal and affectionate with close friends and family
- Independent
- Loves to think about abstract concepts

Weaknesses

- Insensitive
- Free-spirited
- Difficult to understand most of the times

- Easily doubts themselves

Career Paths

Since INTPs favor abstract concepts and theories, they often do well in the field of science and mathematics. Their excellent logical and reasoning skills enable them to be successful in their respective jobs.

These people give a great deal of emphasis on personal independence and autonomy. Sometimes, they clash with authority figures especially when they feel that these people suppress their ability to think and act freely. The "thinkers" shine best in these careers:

- Forensic scientist
- Geologist
- Chemist
- Physicist
- Mathematician
- Pharmacist
- Engineer

- Software developer

Famous People with INFP Personalities

- Tiger Woods
- Albert Einstein
- US Pres. Abraham Lincoln

ESTP (Extraverted, Sensing, Thinking, Perceiving): The Persuader

People who fall under this category enjoy being with their acquaintances and friends. They are conscious of details and are present-focused. When confronted with problems, ESTPs immediately consider the facts on hand and devise a solution from them. They are also known to be "fast talkers" as they have the ability to persuade.

Strengths

- Energetic
- Has a good sense of humor
- Friendly

- Influential
- Action-oriented
- Observant
- Resourceful

Weaknesses

- Overly competitive
- Abhors monotony
- Insensitive
- Impulsive
- Insincere at times

Career Paths

ESTP are energetic individuals who dislike boredom and love being with people. Therefore, they highly favor fast-paced careers like:

- Marketer
- Sales agent
- Paramedics
- Police officer
- Entrepreneur

- Detective

Famous People with INFP Personalities

- US Pres. Donald Trump
- Thomas Edison
- Madonna

ESTJ (Extraverted, Sensing, Thinking, Judging): The Director

From the epithet, "The Director," these people like to take charge of most situations. They make sure that everything works according to the rules and regulations. They are committed to laws, traditions, and standards. They also hold strong beliefs and assume that others will do the same.

Strengths

- Realistic and practical
- Confident
- Traditional
- Have strong leadership skills
- Dependable

Weaknesses

- Inflexible and insensitive
- Bossy
- Antagonistic at times

Career Paths

ESTJs are great in supervisory roles or in careers that maintain peace and order. They strive hard to follow as well as implement the rules set by the government or society. Below are some of the most suitable careers for this personality type:

- School administrator
- Judge
- Business manager
- Accountant
- Banker
- Military
- Police officer

Famous People with INFP Personalities

- Billy Graham

- Terry Bradshaw
- Alec Baldwin

ESFP (Extraverted, Sensing, Feeling, Perceiving): The Performer

ESFPs are known to be spontaneous and outgoing. They're usually considered as class clowns and entertainers. Moreover, they're practical learners and have a great understanding of their environment.

Strengths

- Gregarious and optimistic
- Sociable
- Present-focused

Weaknesses

- Dislikes abstract thinking
- Impulsive
- Hates monotony

Career Paths

These people abhor the monotony of routine. They seek jobs that involve socializing since they feel energized being with the crowd. They find it hard to be happy in jobs that require too much structure or where you have to work alone, which is why these jobs are suitable for ESFPs:

- Actor
- Artist
- Fashion designer
- Musician
- Athletic coach
- A social worker or childcare provider
- Human resource specialist
- Counselor or psychologist

Famous People with INFP Personalities

- Pablo Picasso
- Will Smith
- Elvis Presley

ESFJ (Extraverted, Sensing, Feeling, Judging): The Caregiver

People under this category are fiercely loyal, tender-hearted, sociable, and organized. They gain energy by simply interacting with other people and they also impart their energy by encouraging others to do their best. They always think the best of others and easily give their trust. About nine to thirteen percent of the population are considered ESFJs.

Strengths

- Gregarious
- Outgoing
- Kind and dependable
- Finds pleasure in helping others

Weaknesses

- People pleaser
- Sensitive to criticism

Career Paths

ESFJ people feel at home in the field of social and health care services or in jobs that need their support and dependability. Thus, these jobs prove to be appropriate:

- Bookkeeper
- Receptionist
- Office manager
- Childcare provider
- Nurse
- Teacher
- Social worker
- Counselor
- Physician

Famous People with INFP Personalities

- Danny Glover
- Sally Struthers

ENFP (Extraverted, Intuitive, Feeling, Perceiving): The Champion

ENFPs are described as charismatic, vivacious, and innovative. There are about five to seven percent of people that fall into this category. Furthermore, these people dislike routines and tend to focus on the future.

Strengths

- Strong communication skills
- Empathetic
- Strong interpersonal skills
- Open and fun to be with

Weaknesses

- People pleaser
- Dramatic
- Tend to overthink
- Find it hard to follow rules
- Easily stressed out

Career Paths

As mentioned, ENFPs bear a great deal of charisma and interpersonal skills. These jobs come highly recommended for this type:

- Psychologist

- Journalist
- TV Anchor/Reporter
- Politician
- Counselor

Famous People with INFP Personalities

- Dr. Seuss
- Bob Dylan
- Joseph Campbell

ENFJ (Extraverted, Intuitive, Feeling, Judging): The Giver

Strengths

- Empathetic
- Friendly and encouraging
- Organized

Weaknesses

- Overly sensitive
- Indecisive
- Approval-seeking

Career Paths

The ENFJs' strong organizational and interpersonal skills make them befitting in the following careers:

- Counselor
- Teacher
- Human resources manager
- Manager

Famous People with INFP Personalities

- Abraham Maslow
- US President Barack Obama

ENTP (Extraverted, Intuitive, Thinking, Perceiving): The Debater

ENTPs are also known as "the innovator" or "the visionary." They are expressive and clever, never running out of ideas and theories.

Strengths

- Great debaters and conversationalists
- Highly value knowledge

Weaknesses

- Unfocused
- Strongly dislike being controlled
- Argumentative
- Insensitive

Career Paths

These people are nonconformists and do their best in jobs filled with excitement and creativity. Hence, the following jobs suit them best:

- Lawyer
- Inventor or scientist
- Journalist
- Engineer

Famous People with INFP Personalities

- Walt Disney
- Alexander the Great

ENTJ (Extraverted, Intuitive, Thinking, Judging): The Commander

This personality type is quite rare, consisting merely two percent of the entire population. These people have strong verbal and decision-making skills. They also tend to focus on the future instead of the here-and-now.

Strengths

- Great in planning and organizing
- Strong leadership skills
- Assertive
- Confident

Weaknesses

- Impatient and stubborn
- Aggressive
- Intolerant

Career Paths

ENTJs strive in a work environment that requires lots of structure and lets them interact with various people. They excel in jobs where they can exercise their leadership and planning skills like:

- Entrepreneur
- Company CEO
- University professor
- Lawyer
- Business analyst

Famous People with INFP Personalities

- Bill Gates
- UK Prime Minister Margaret Thatcher
- Al Gore

Chapter 7: Learning, Recognizing, and Reading Hidden Body Messages

Body language accounts for up to more than half of how we communicate, but reading and analyzing nonverbal cues are not just about broad strokes. A certain gesture can have a number of different meanings depending on the context. Now, let's take a look at some situations where understanding these nonverbal cues or what we call body language is significant:

- Going out on a Date
- Detecting Lies
- Going on an Interview

When you are able to interpret body language accurately, you can read beyond what the other person is willing to tell you or when their words do not convey what the person honestly feels.

We lie a lot with our words. Most of the time we tell lies to save ourselves from embarrassment or penalties. Once we start telling a lie, it may lead to more lies. The lies we tell may not be big, but considered white lies, yet, we're still lying, and we willingly partake in deception from time to time to avoid conflict. However, can possibility get out of trouble with words, but our bodies are TERRIBLE LIARS! This is where reading and analyzing body language can be extremely useful when communicating with others.

When reading body language, it is your primary duty to determine whether the individual is comfortable or not in their present situation. There are many ways to determine a person's comfort level, and here are some of them:

Positive Body Language

- Relaxed and with uncrossed limbs
- Leaning closer to you
- Long periods of eye contact
- A genuine smile

Negative Body Language

- Moving or leaning away from you

- Crossed arms and legs
- Looking away
- Feet pointed towards the exit
- Rubbing or scratching the nose, rubbing the eyes or the back of the neck.

A single act can mean a thousand other things. For instance, crossed arms indicates a negative body language. It can, likewise, tell you that the person is feeling physically cold, frustrated, or closed off. Nonetheless, it can also mean that the person may have eaten too much, and something is happening in the digestive system. It is, therefore, necessary to pay attention to multiple behavioral cues than just concentrate on a single cue as it is often misleading.

While it helps to determine a person's comfort level to accurately read their behavior, you need to look deeper. Meaning, you also have to pay attention to other cues as well as their context. As we take a look into some specific situations, we'll see how these cues will work together to help divulge the underlying truth in any given situation.

Knowing When Someone is Lying

One of the biggest benefits you can get from being able to read body language is being able to judge accurately when someone is lying. Our intuition is not 100% accurate, but with little practice, you will become more aware when someone is trying to feed you a load of crap. It's also very important that you determine what kind of lies they're telling you.

We will discuss lies that make people uncomfortable to tell the truth. With this skill, you can easily detect white lies, lies of omission, or exaggerated stories. This type of deception is very difficult to spot and so you always need to remember that regardless of what type of lies, you will never know for certain. Nonetheless, you can spot common cues that will let you know when to suspect that person is lying.

The author of the *Liespotting* conducted a study on the different ways people lie in order to determine a pattern in our body language. She was able to define through the study that liars often display much of the behavior you would find in a person who feels uncomfortable, although there are a few more additional traits.

It is said that a *Duchenne smile* or a smile that is genuine is almost impossible to fake, which is why most people end up having awkward smiles in most photos. When you think you're you have a great smile, others may think you're faking it.

A smile is seen fake if it doesn't reach your eyes. When your smile is genuine, the areas around your eyes will wrinkle because your smile automatically pushes up your cheeks and crinkles the skin near your eyes, making it hard to fake.

A real smile comes from within and shows in your eyes, which is impossible to do when you are feeling uncomfortable. It is why a non-genuine smile is a helpful way to indicate a lie.

It's a common knowledge that guilt can be seen in someone's eyes when they're lying. To overcompensate this, great liars tried their best to stay calm and offer steady eye contact. This didn't work because the liars tried not to fidget, and they stiffened their bodies.

Generally, people can't keep eye contact for long periods of time. When eye contact becomes uncomfortable, people will rub their eyes or neck and tend to look away. So, instead of exhibiting body language that implies comfort, liars would opt to do very little, which is an indicator in itself. To spot a liar, look for unusually long eye contact and tense shoulders.

Aside from all these nonverbal cues, you also need to pay attention to the context or the setting that forms the event in order to gain a full understanding of the whole situation. Liars will often offer more details than necessary, suggest punishment, and prefer to answer your question with a question, which can give them time to fabricate an answer that will hide the truth. Such behavior, when paired with the standard negative body language and cues that liars normally exhibit, will give you the right blend of behavior that should not be trusted. Separately, they won't mean much but together, they can only mean one thing - DISHONESTY.

It is important, however, to remember that there are people who are just awkward and could display such behavior. You must take into consideration the normal behavior of a person. Watch out for their eye movements and mannerisms when you know they are telling the truth and compare it to their usual responses whenever they are lying.

If you observed a lot of inconsistencies, you will know how an individual acts when they are thinking of what to say rather than recalling information. Again, this is not enough, along with anything previously mentioned to detect lies. You, therefore, have to look for multiple cues to know the difference between fact and fiction.

Reading People on a Date

Body language can be an incredible tool when you're out on your first date with someone. If you neglect to pay attention to verbal cues your date is exhibiting, you can possibly do something that will make them uncomfortable. While you may not want to go out on a date hiding the real you, starting with your best foot forward is the best way to begin any relationship in case you find out later that you are a decent match.

This requires paying close attention to your date's behavior, which is not easy when you are trying to impress your date with your charm. Nonetheless, with more practice, you'll get the hang of watching out for the right signals.

Remember that you are not looking for anything too complicated on your first date but just basic indications of comfort and discomfort. Simply put, pay attention to how your date is guarding their body. In the beginning, most people will feel fairly guarded. They will cross their arms with palms facing them and keep a reasonable amount of distance. This is quite common especially on the first date but if you like your date, your goal is to alter that body language into something more open and welcoming to ease the situation and make you both comfortable.

In some extent, we tend to mimic the behavior of others. If you feel comfortable, it will help your date change his or her behavior to match yours. This means, you should simply avoid crossing your arms and try offering a genuine smile when appropriate and feasible. Avoid distancing yourself from your date or even showing your palms to imply that you are comfortable, which will help your date be more comfortable as well.

Also, remember not to lose your patience when you detect some negative cues as levels of comfort frequently fluctuates on dates, which is usually nerve-wracking for most people. As most piano instructors will tell you on your recital, if you happen to play the wrong note, just keep going and don't worry about making mistakes. Look out for positive signs to see how your date reacts to you and focus on providing positive body language. If you continue to see negative cues, move on to another topic.

Sometimes, both of you aren't going to click and your date may exhibit many negative cues. If this happens, apply the same piano recital principle, which is to move on and don't get hung up on a problem.

Communicating Effectively in an Interview

Interviews are like first dates. You are trying to convince a person you've met for the first time to like you. However, unlike dating, an interviewer is on a different level. This alone is enough to create an environment of discomfort that can force you to display negative cues, which are not helpful. When interviewing for a job, you should avoid using body language that makes you seem closed off.

Creating a good first impression is vital in hiring decisions. So, smile pleasantly, provide a firm handshake, and properly greet the interviewer. This positive body language will set the stage for a comfortable interview that will follow. You are not aware of the expectations the interviewer will bring to the table, so it's a good idea to avoid any negative behavior by demonstrating your pleasant and charismatic personality.

Nonetheless, offering all those positive cues is easier said than done when you are feeling uncomfortable in the first place. The best thing to do is prepare before the interview. Usually, lack of preparation is the reason why people do poorly in interviews.

As preparation, research the company. An interviewer expects you to have prior knowledge of the company you want to join. Anticipate some questions that are often included in a job interview like:

- Why should they choose you over the other candidates?
- How can you help the company?
- What salary are your salary requirements?

Walking into the room with confidence is vital in creating a good first impression. Remember that you need to stand out from the crowd. When you are well-prepared to face your interview, this breeds confidence and your body automatically exhibits positive body language when you're feeling good about yourself.

While natural comfort is what you actually need, there are some tricks that can help you out when you need it. As an American cultural standard, eye contact is more important in a job interview than in most other situation. If you have trouble staring into someone's eyes, your next best option is to look at their mouth.

Like when you're on a date, leaning forward is a positive cue you can provide to your interviewer. It makes you appear a good listener even when you have to talk most of the time. When asking some questions or when your interviewer is saying something, eye contact is vital. This conveys that you are in the listening mode. Occasionally placing your hand over your mouth indicates that you aren't going to talk and are not paying attention.

The interviewer is used to small signs of nervousness and they can understand when you have it. So, when you're a bit tense on your interview, there's no need to worry about it. That is usually expected. In fact, too much comfort might convey overconfidence and not taking the interview seriously. In the end, your fate lies in the decision made by another person and there's only so much that you can do to impress the person.

They may not like the way you dress or prefer to hire someone else but with the help of your skill in reading and manipulating body language, you can at least try to tip the scale in your favor.

Reading Power Cues

Eye Contact is usually the primary way to communicate dominance. People establish dominance by taking the liberty to stare and scrutinize others while making direct eye contact. A dominant person is usually the last to break eye contact.

So, if you intend to assert your power, remember that constant eye contact can also be intimidating.

Assess Facial Expressions

A dominant person or a person in power refrains from smiling to relay seriousness. They would prefer to purge their lips instead or frown.

Evaluate Gesture and Stance

Pointing a finger at someone and using large gestures are examples of exhibiting dominance.

When a person uses a taller and wider stance while being relaxed, it shows dominance.

Dominant individuals also have firm handshakes and usually place a hand on top with the palm facing downwards. The grip of this person is firm and sustained to demonstrate power and control.

Managing Personal Space

People in power or high status basically enable more physical space between themselves and people below their rank or status. This is to show dominance and mastery in every situation. Simply put, an expansive pose is a sign of power and achievement.

Power is likewise displayed in a standing position against those sitting down. Standing is seen to emit power than the sitting pose.

A straight back while keeping shoulders back instead of leaning forward further displays confidence. In contrast, slouching and slumping shows a lack of confidence.

A person of dominance also leads from the front and chooses to walk ahead of anyone especially in a group. They like to be in front and go through the door first.

The Way of Touching

Those who assert their status are likely to have more options when it comes to touching because they feel more confident of their position and authority. Generally, in a situation where two individuals have unequal status, the one occupying the higher status is likely to touch with greater frequency than the one with lower status.

Chapter 8: Knowledge and Techniques Required to Understand and Interpret Body Language

Because the majority of our communication is made through body language, it is, therefore, crucial to pay attention to it—especially when at work. This is where your emotional intelligence comes in.

How Body Language is Connected to Emotional Quotient (EQ)

Emotional Quotient is the sum of the following:

- Self-awareness
- Self-management
- Social awareness
- Relationship management

All of these elements are significant to body language.

Self-Awareness

Be mindful of your voice or tone, as well as your posture, so that you deliver the message in a way appropriate to the situation.

Social Awareness

Understanding other person's body language is, likewise, vital to how you would act in a certain situation.

Self-Management

As the situation changes, you must pay attention to the mitigating changes in your body language.

Relationship Management

This is about changing your body language and adjusting your message to suit every situation.

However, none of these is useful unless we understand the meaning behind the body language. Here is some of the common body language often used in the workplace:

Confident

- Face is relaxed
- Solid eye contact
- Firm handshake
- Walking with purpose
- Hand movements are wide and open
- Arms open

Nervous or Uncertain

- Face tight and tensed
- Avoid holding eye contact
- Movements of the hands are jerky
- Arms are folded across chest
- Walking is not stable or tentative
- Handshake is weak

Defensive

- No eye contact, eyes are downcast
- Hand gestures are closer to the body
- Arms crossed or folded over chest
- Facial expression is neutral

- The body is turned away from you

Bored and Inattentive

- Head is down
- Glazed eyes
- Slumped when sitting in a chair
- No eye contact; Eyes are somewhere else
- Hands are fidgeting
- Thinking (Prior to responding)

Thinking (Prior to Responding)

- Head tilted on an angle while eyes looking at a distance
- Hand on the cheek
- Fingers are either resting on the chin
- Broken eye contact. Eyes return only when something is asked

Harvard psychologist, Amy Cuddy, researched the impact of body language on an individual's confidence, influence, and success. Her findings dwell on the potent effects of positive body language.

Studies show that people with positive body language are more competent, persuasive, likable, and possess a higher level of emotional intelligence.

Let's find out how positive body language works.

It Changes Behavior and Attitude

Cuddy suggests that adjusting your body language to make it more positive has a powerful impact on your hormones, which improves your attitude.

It Increases Testosterone

When thinking of testosterone, you are probably thinking more of those manly hormones commonly used in competitive sports. However, testosterone is more than sports. In fact, it covers much more. Testosterone works to improve anyone's confidence—in both men and women, which causes other people to see you as someone who is positive and trustworthy. Research also proves that positive body language increases your testosterone levels by 20%.

It Decreases Cortisol

Another stress hormone that impedes performance and creates negative effects on your health over time is cortisol. By decreasing levels of cortisol, it minimizes stress and enables you to have a clear mind particularly when facing challenging and difficult situations. Studies, likewise, prove that positive body language decreases cortisol levels by at least 25%.

It Creates a Powerful Combination

While increased testosterone and decreased cortisol can do wonders on their own, when combined, it results in a powerful combination that is often found in people who are in a position of power. This combination creates confidence and clarity of the mind that is a significant requirement for dealing with pressure brought on by tight deadlines, making tough decisions, and massive workloads.

People who have high testosterone levels and are low in cortisol are known to survive under pressure. You can develop positive body language even when you don't have these natural gifts.

It Makes you More Likeable

Body language is a big factor in how you are perceived by others and is more important than your voice, tone, or the message you're trying to impart. Using positive language, therefore, can influence people to like and trust you more.

Ways to Gauge EQ Through Body Language

Now that you are aware of how EQ is strongly linked to body language, you can see how EQ development is essential to acquire a set of positive body language that can help you achieve a better, happier, and successful life in the future.

Our body contains thoughts as well as emotions and conveys messages that other people pick up to use and make judgments on us. Becoming aware of those messages that our body is sending is crucial to our success in all areas of life. By being aware of what our body does, we can manipulate the messages that it is sending so that they will cause the impact we intend.

Here are ways emotional intelligence is conveyed in body language:

Handshakes

Handshakes are basically important as they leave indelible impressions of us to others. A handshake that is weak leaves an impression of a lack of confidence and interest. Conversely, bone-crushing handshakes send red flags of an aggressive individual with the tendency to be dominant. When doing a handshake, meet the other person's eyes when possible as this can leave a lasting impression. People with high EQ know the right amount of pressure to use appropriately in every situation.

Giving Appropriate Space

The amount of appropriate space where one can be comfortable varies in every culture. If you stand too close to a person you just met, it can be uncomfortable for them and emits a signal of aggressiveness and dominance while standing too far from the person is a sign that you are uncomfortable with the person or you lack the confidence you need.

Facing Others Squarely

When you aren't squaring your body when conversing or turning away from the person you are speaking to indicates that you are either uninterested or uncomfortable. This can be a sign of disrespect or being impolite.

Positive body language involves parallel shoulder and foot placement mirroring that of the other person. People who have high EQ levels usually lean towards the person they are talking to. This means that they are giving them their complete and undivided attention.

What Posture Suggests

Standing straight or sitting up while speaking is a power position. They are an indication of confidence and self-respect as well as showing interest in what the other person is saying. Simply put, they value the conversation.

On the other hand, slouching indicates the opposite such as the lack of serious intent on whatever the other person is saying. It also suggests that you don't care how the other person views you; it can be a sign of a lack of self-esteem.

Shutting Out Distractions

We have experienced at one time or another a person who is checking their watch or mobile phone while engaging in a conversation. This makes us want to end the discussion. It is apparent that the other person is not interested in whatever it is that you're saying and has a more interesting thing to do than listen to you. People with high EQ are constantly on guard against this kind of behavior and the message it implies. To avoid this, fight the habit to look at your watch or device when you are talking to someone.

Appropriate Eye Contact

Failing to have eye contact can arouse suspicion that you are hiding something. Looking down when someone is telling you something can be regarded as a lack of confidence or interest. However, intense, sustained eye contact implies aggressiveness or wanting to dominate although there are cultural variations. Those with great EQ levels, however, tend to maintain eye contact for a few seconds to convey respect for the other person and keep the conversation focused. It is vital to glance to the side instead of the floor to avoid being perceived as uninterested.

Unconscious Microexpressions

A smile to start up a conversation can warm the heart but when it's unnatural, it may cause suspicion as well as question the sincerity of the person.

A pleasant neutral expression is much better than forcing a smile you don't feel. Scowling or having a serious expression can convey hostility causing others to get defensive and uncomfortable.

Having the right body language is just as important as using words with the appropriate tone of voice when speaking to others. Just like any other habit, it comes down to practicing until it becomes natural as you acquire the skill.

Chapter 9: Reading and Understanding Different Cues

Reading nonverbal behavior is a complex task since it involves people and every individual is unique and presents themselves differently. The task of reading body language can be challenging because you are trying to interpret the signs sent by people. One can't read and understand what's behind a certain action without taking into account the whole picture.

In interpreting other people's body language, you have to take into account the following:

- Personality
- Social factors
- Verbal behavior
- Setting

While the information presented isn't always complete and in some other circumstances not available, reading body language can be useful. Because people are complex, it shouldn't come as a surprise that the way they convey themselves through their bodies.

The Mouth

Another physical aspect that is significant in reading body language is the mouth. Habits like chewing on the bottom lip can show that the person is worried, insecure, fearful or anxious. Even smiles can be interpreted in many ways. It can be a genuine smile, or an attempt to cover up the person's real feeling. It can also be a sign of cynicism.

Once you feel that you are about to cough or yawn, your hand automatically covers your mouth. Nonetheless, there are people who do this as an attempt to cover any facial expressions showing disapproval.

When trying to assess a person's body language, pay attention to the following lip and mouth signals:

Pursed Lips

- The tightening of the lips is evident of distrust, dislike, and disapproval.
- Biting the lips indicates being stressed, worried, or anxious
- The mouth that is either turned up or down can be a sullen indication of what the person is feeling at the moment. If the mouth is vaguely turned up, it is an indication of happiness. However, when the mouth is slightly turn downward, it means that the person might be sad. It can also be a sign of disapproval or an outright grimace.

Gestures

This is the clearest and obvious of all body signals. It is common to see someone waving, pointing or raising a hand to get someone's attention. Using hands to indicate numbers is also widely used all over the world and it is easily recognized by people in the different regions, states, or countries.

There are some cultural signs that are considered a positive sign in one region but abominable to others. An example of this is the circling of the thumb and index finger as a sign of money. It is not appropriate to use this hand signal when you are in Japan or in the Middle East countries as they consider it an abominable behavior.

When it comes to reading body language accurately, you need to consider individual differences. There's no one-size-fits-all policy. Hence, if you are interested in studying an individual, you need to take some time to do it. What holds true for one person may not necessarily hold true to another.

For instance, it is a common for liars to avoid eye contact because of guilt. This may be true to some but there are people who manage to master this skill to get away with telling lies.

Body language varies according to culture.

- In the Finnish culture, making eye contact symbolizes that a person is easy to approach. In contrast, Japanese culture this is an expression of anger.

- Westerners easily lean forward and square their faces and bodies towards you when they are comfortable.

- Autistic people also have their own unique body language. When listening, they avoid eye contact and play with their hands.

While body language differs from culture to culture, there are certain nonverbal expressions that are universal and common to all cultures like smiling to signify friendliness and a lowered posture to indicate submission.

Understanding body language differs according to nonverbal communication channels. The nonverbal channel refers to the means by which a cue or message is relayed without the use of words. Significant nonverbal channels include those of kinesics (eye contact, body language, and facial expressions), haptic (touch), and proxemics (personal space). In simple words, it's the medium that determines the message.

As a general rule, people can easily read facial expressions, and then body language, before personal space and touch. Even within the same channel, there are variations. To illustrate, not all facial expressions are easy to read and understand. People are generally better at reading pleasant facial expressions than unpleasant ones. There is a study that stated individuals are better in accurately reading contentment, happiness, and excitement compared to disgust, fear, and sadness.

In interpreting verbal and nonverbal cues, you want to read a person beyond what you can see. Logic alone won't tell you the whole story of what is behind a person's facade. You must learn to surrender to other vital forms of information so you can learn to read and understand the important non-verbal intuitive cues that people emit unconsciously. To do this, you need to rid yourself of any preconceptions and emotional baggage such as resentments, prejudice, or clashes of ego that hinders you from seeing someone clearly.

While reading other people—your partner or anyone with accuracy, keep away from biases. Regardless of how brilliant the intellect is, you have to let go of limiting ideas. People trained to read others are trained to read what is unseen or invisible so they can utilize their super senses. Most of the time, this requires surrendering pure logic in favor of receiving non-linear forms of alternative inputs.

Here are useful body language techniques in reading cues.

In this technique, try hard not to read body language cues and try not to be intense or analytical. Instead, stay relaxed and fluid. Be comfortable, simply sit back and observe.

Focus on the Person's Appearance

- Take note of the style and color of the clothes they're wearing
- Do they dress for success?
- Do they dress for comfort?
- Do they dress for seduction?
- Are they wearing anything to indicate spiritual values like a cross pendant?

Notice the Posture

When trying to analyze posture, take note of the following:

- Do they hold their head high? (confidence)
- Do they walk with indecisive steps? (low self-esteem)
- Do they swagger when they walk (arrogance)

Analyze Body Expressions and Facial Expressions

Isn't it interesting how two people can converse without actually speaking? Body language has played an important role especially in the world of dating. The laws of attraction revolve around body language. A man and a woman can express their attraction to the opposite sex through physical action or gestures and facial expressions.

Emotional Cues

Noticing the signals that other people are sending and accurately understanding them is a very useful skill one needs to learn. With a little sensitivity, attentiveness, and practice you can develop this habit and it can become second nature to you.

Crying

Crying is the same across all cultures. It is a sign of sadness or grief. At times, crying can also be a sign of joy and happiness. Crying is sometimes associated with laughter. So when evaluating crying, you need to look for other signals to determine its appropriate context.

While emotions can be manipulated in general, so is crying to gain sympathy or as a tool for deception. We call this "crocodile tears"—a colloquial term that draws on the myth that crocodiles do cry when catching prey.

Anger or Threat

When you see a person with eyebrows drawn in a V-shape accompanied with wide eyes and a down-turned mouth, expect that person to be angry.

Other signs common in an angry individual are arms tightly crossed and the person being closed off.

Anxiety

A person suffering from anxiety can be detected by fidgeting hands that they can't seem to control or keep in place. This person also unconsciously taps their feet to cope up with the feeling of restlessness.

Embarrassment

When a person is embarrassed, they tend to avert their eyes, and turn their head away with a controlled or a tense smile.

If a person is timid and shy, they may focus their attention on the floor. People who are upset also behave this way when trying to hide an emotion. When they are thinking or experiencing unpleasant emotions, they tend to stare at the ground.

Proud or Boastful

People display pride by smiling a little with the head tilted backward, and hands on their hips.

Attraction Cues

When a group of people were asked about the best tip on flirting, their answer was reading body language. So now, let's focus on the common attraction cues usually evident in women.

A woman that draws attention to her lips is indeed sending a strong sensual signal. This can be her subtle way of telling the guy how he strongly attracts her. Other cues may involve wetting her lips, eating something slowly or putting on lipstick. Through this body language, she is saying that she wants to have some fun with you.

Another indication that a woman is sexually interested in you is when she is playing with her glass using her fingers. Usually, this occurs in bars or night clubs. It is not just a habit but a form of teasing or tempting the man.

When a woman swings her legs while sitting cross-legged, it indicates that she is in a sexual mood.

However, there is unconscious body language and women may not be aware they are sending a sexual cue. This occurs a woman claspes her hands and places them over her stomach. It is a way of telling others that she is fertile and ready to conceive.

When women are showing you positive signs of sexual attraction, she can, likewise, send out cues to show disinterest in an individual. When women talk to you with arms crossed, this means she is not interested in you or in having a conversation with you. They are crossing their arms over their chest because they feel threatened, which means she has a preconceived idea of distrust towards you.

If women are sending sexual cues, what about guys? Are they sending the same cues?

The answer is YES! Men, like women, know how to use different body language and the most common one is inserting a thumb in their pants pocket or placing their hands over the crotch of their pants. Unconsciously, men are showing off their crotch area to attract potential sexual mates.

Another indicator of attraction is the seating position. You may not be aware of it, however, in a large group of people, we can identify who we are attracted to if our bodies are facing the person. Even when someone else engages us in a conversation, we simply turn our heads in response but retain our body position.

On the negative side, if the man chooses to play with his watch while talking with a woman, it indicates that he is forming a barrier with his arms. It could be that he finds it uncomfortable to have the woman around or he could also be nervous engaging with her. So for women, I suggest that you try to be a bit more friendly and lively when you find your date acting this way.

There are countless body languages used for flirting and both men and women are using them in their everyday life. Learning how body language can help you find a romantic partner proves to be useful most of the time.

Relational Cues

Body language can say much about what's happening in a relationship. Whether one partner is feeling distant, having second thoughts about something, or will is excited to go home to be with you.

The clues are actually written all over your partner's body language. All you need to do is to be aware of your partner's actions and be sensitive to what you have learned about nonverbal cues. Now, there's more to what you have learned in previous chapters.

Walking

When walking with your partner, you walk side by side at the same pace and if the intimacy is quite strong, it's most likely that you hold hands while walking. In psychology, when two individuals have rapport, their movements are in sync. One can, therefore, be a mirror of the other.

So when couples are walking and one is walking ahead of the other or lagging behind, it's a warning sign that they lack rapport. The one who is walking ahead means he or she wants to lead or get away from the partner or relationship while the one lagging behind is either scared of the relationship or feel intimidated by the partner. If one partner crosses the street without any verbal or nonverbal signs, it can indicate something negative.

Sitting

When sitting, intimate couples sit next to each other and not across from one another. Note that couples with positive body language make an effort to connect all the time regardless of what they are doing or where they are. Couples with good body language will face each other, have eye contact, hold hands, kiss or hug each other when not engaging in a conversation. When there are distractions, their attention is diverted but they reengage after a while. Even when eating, couples tend to eat in proportion to each other.

Negative signs are when there isn't a connection between couples. They busy themselves by reading the menu, looking out of the window, watching passersby, and using their mobile phones. Their bodies are usually angled away from each other and there is minimal body contact. One can be eating a lot while the other one is barely touching their meal. The one who barely touches the plate probably thinking of other things.

Making Love

When couples are deeply connected with each other, it can be deeper than just the physical level. There is always that strong mental connection that occurs especially when making love. Eye contact is vital—both partners should freely look into each other's eyes during lovemaking. Clasping of the hands, eye contact, touching skin to skin and kissing helps form a much deeper connection.

Conversely, negative signs in lovemaking are reflected in the closed eye as well as stiffness in the neck and shoulders. These are signs of ongoing anxiety or coldness in emotion. Sometimes, it can be a sign of guilt.

One must be aware of the nonverbal communication you receive from your partner rather than the verbal communication. According to Albert Mehrabian, a psychologist, it's not what you say that matters but how you say it.

Chapter 10: Understanding Non-Verbal Cues for Success in Career and Business

Are you aware that you have this inherent ability to see what goes on in the minds of other people? Reading other people's thoughts is not actually a magic trick but can be accomplished by deeply observing their microexpressions.

Microexpressions to be Aware of When Negotiating

Microexpressions are displays of emotions that are evidently seen through facial expressions. They occur and last for less than a second before the brain has the chance to alter the displayed emotion. Therefore, the displayed emotion is a genuine reaction to the stimulus that caused the display of emotion.

There are microexpressions that are common to everyone regardless of location. That means the reaction to a certain stimulus would be the same wherever you are or whatever culture you belong to.

Anger

It is natural for people to get upset. When a person loses control, it can turn into anger. So when in a negotiation, be mindful of the other person's temperament. Once he loses his coolness, that's the time when he becomes irritable and irrational. Manipulation can be easy at this time. So if you know how to take this to your advantage, then this can be a real opportunity for you to win the negotiation.

Fear

Fear is a sort of defense mechanism as we tend to protect ourselves although fear can be debilitating. When in a negotiation, it will be to your advantage if you can detect this sense of fear in your negotiating opponent. To use this to your advantage, you have to know what makes him fearful.

The following are apparent in a person feeling a genuine fear:

- Raised eyebrows
- Parted lips with bottom lips protruding downward

Between fear and anger, there are two major differences. The eyebrows are raised when the person is experiencing fear and lowered when angry with flaring of nostrils like an angry bull.

Disgust

When the other negotiator says "yes" to the offer but you notice that his upper lip is lifted with nose turned up in a wrinkle, then he just displayed the microexpression of disgust. You must take note of the difference between his words and his actions as his statement of agreement is not as firm as his body language indicates.

Surprise

A surprise expression can either be good or bad. A surprised expression is manifested by wide eyes, raised eyebrows, and a mouth that's partly open. Note that these are common in fear and surprise expressions.

It is important to notice if the expression of surprise is due to happy or sad expectations. If someone is extremely happy about a negotiation that you offered, scale back on your emotions. Your goal is to win the negotiation so you may have to make adjustments.

When in a negotiation, observe if the surprise act stemmed from either happy or sad expectations. When your offer proves to be too advantageous than what was expected, consider a reduction.

Contempt

This gesture is often conveyed by a sneer, e.g., with one corner of the mouth turned upward. Note that this may lead to disgust and then anger. In a negotiation, this microexpression may suggest one thing, "I am not enjoying this" or "this is insulting!"

Sadness

Dropping eyelids with lips turned down and a change in voice tone and pitch indicate sadness in the person. It could be that the person realizes that you have the upper hand and left little room to negotiate. If this is the case, you should avoid turning sadness into anger, which may eventually lead to a negative response.

Happiness

This is evident in a person's smile, wide-eyes, raised cheeks, and manifested gaiety.

When perceiving happiness, take note what caused it but don't let your guard down. If it's real, everything will be smooth, but it could also be an attempt to lull you into a false sense of security. Good negotiators are looking for an advantage in every negotiation and this microexpression can be the advantage you need.

When in negotiations, reading people's body language can give you insights and, therefore, be very useful. If you are able to read the thoughts and interpret your opponent's gestures, it will give you an additional advantage on the deal. Once you're able to read and analyze body language with a high degree of accuracy, you will be on your way to achieving what you have come for.

Have you ever experienced any situation when you were able to tell what someone is going to say even before words were said? How were you able to do this? You may not be aware of it, but this is actually the because your mind is mentally synchronized with another person's mind. The same thing works when someone else tells you that they have a strong feeling that you are going to say something they see in their mind. It is because your aura allows someone to hear your unspoken thoughts or see hidden chambers of your mind?

Reading Body Language to Win Negotiations

When you are negotiating, are you aware that you can negotiate better by reading the body language of the other person? The secret to reading the body language better is to know what signals to look for and how to interpret and use these signals to your advantage.

Before negotiations, take time to learn the skill of reading cues unconsciously relayed by the other party. The benefit of accurate reading and assessment of these cues can result in you winning the deal you are after.

When you are sitting at the negotiating table, allow the other negotiator to see your facade. Having the skill to read body language, likewise, provides you with the knowledge of manipulating your own body language to your advantage.

When the other negotiator reads your body language the way you want them to see, they will think they have the advantage.

Body Signals to Look for in a Negotiation

In addition to covering up your real intentions through your body language, you observe your opponent's nonverbal cues to enhance your negotiation efforts. For better negotiation results, observe your opponent. Here are some of the things you have to look out for when observing the other party.

Creases at the Forehead

Apparent creases (unnatural wrinkles) on the forehead is a sign of stress and the absence of these creases means that the person is calm and going easy during negotiations.

Eyes

It is important to observe the direction of the eyes of the other negotiator to assess information. Eyes opened wide indicate interest and attentiveness while being open-minded. On the contrary, narrowing of the eyes signals a higher degree of focus on the subject.

To gain an accurate assessment of their eye movements, you first need to establish a baseline. Do this while in a non-threatening environment prior to the official negotiation. To establish a baseline, you should ask questions pertaining to an everyday situation like:

- How is the weather today?
- How long have you been in this business?
- Do you like watching sports?

Ask questions that may allow the other person to think about their answers so you can observe eye movements—Is the movement towards the left, or right? Is the person looking upward or downward? Follow up with other non-threatening questions to confirm how the person's eyes move when trying to recall something.

Speech Pace

Another aspect that you need to closely observe in the other person is their speech pace. How fast or how slow is the person speaking? Generally, people's normal pace is between 110-150 words per minute. As a person gets more excited, this can increase to 175-240 words per minute. This rate also suggests anxiety or discomfort.

To be able to gain insight into the mental perspective of your counterpart to the negotiation, observe the point where his speech tends to quicken and why it occurs at that specific point? Also take note of any moisture on his lips, hands, or brows. These indicate nervousness or anxiety when there is a quickening of speech. Knowing all these can make you maneuver the person either into a heightened state of agitation or calmness, whichever suits your objective at the time of the negotiation.

Hand Movements

It helps a great deal to observe the body language of someone you are negotiating with especially the movements of the hands. You should learn to observe their hands as hands convey a lot of hidden information in a negotiation.

For example, people use their hands to show appreciation by clapping. Others display their hands to show displeasure. Even while speaking, hand movements give insight into thoughts being processed. So, when someone is speaking, the movement of their hands add or detract the message they are trying to deliver. The same is true when you are conveying information.

Sometimes, you can observe that there's a difference in a person's body language and with their words. If this happens, you have to pay more attention to nonverbal communication. Body language discloses a person's intent more than their words.

Open hand gestures signify that the person is not fearful but when hands are closed like rubbing together or rubbing other parts of the body or getting close to the body, it shows that the person is anxious or too cautious. When you want to make a good impression, keep hands open and avoid making gestures that might be seen as indecisive or not in consonance with your words. Doing so will likely reduce your ability to persuade.

Here are some hands movements that you should lightly consider when conversing with someone but strongly consider when negotiating.

Hand Close to the Body

If the person you are dealing with is guarding their thoughts, you are more likely to find their hands closer to the body. This happens when that person senses threats to their well-being. Their hands are positioned to protect themselves from perceived indifference.

When you see this at the start of any negotiation, it helps to put the other person at ease. You may have to address a point that made the other person uncomfortable before you can induce a positive atmosphere conducive to a winning negotiation.

Hands With Fingers Interlocked

A negotiation displaying hands with interlocking fingers suggests that they are not open to your suggestion, offer or counteroffer.

Once you have obtained the pattern in their eye movements related to when they are recalling information, you will be able to determine if the person is lying or being truthful during the actual negotiation.

To confirm your observation, notice certain acts like having hands with interlocked fingers as this usually implies not being receptive to your offer during negotiations. Take note of the response given. If the person unlocked their fingers, ask them to proceed. In this situation, you have made some changes to their body language and made the person more mentally receptive to you and your offer. Another thing, you have given the person the lead and therefore will highlight what they consider important.

Hands Pushed Away With Palms Out

Take note of this gesture as it implies that the person has no interest in what is being offered. You can, likewise, measure the level of disagreement by the way the palms are pushed outward. You must also be aware of when the other person voices their assertions that are in agreeance with you. Is this case, their body language contradicts real feelings, so believe the gestures more than the words.

Feet

Both feet of parties involved in a negotiation must be facing each other. When one person turns a foot away, it means that a person has disengaged from negotiations and will soon leave.

Touching

The degree of touching between negotiators depends on how they are familiar with each other. Therefore, it is crucial that you are mindful of how you touch the other person. You may not want to be perceived negatively. Take note of how the person reacts when touched. Were they slightly pulling back or flinching? That's a sure sign that you have overstepped the boundary. Pay close attention so you can gauge how you are being received.

Voice and Tone

Be sensitive to the other person's tone especially when there are any changes that occur while negotiating. Ending a sentence with a high pitch can turn a statement into a question. This can make you sound less in authority than what you actually intended.

All of this body language or nonverbal cues can have an impact on how your words can be perceived by the other party. So be mindful of how you deliver your body language more than your words.

Signs that You Have the Other Person's Full Attention

There are signs that indicate the person is listening and absorbing everything that you are saying, which will most likely end things in your favor.

Hands on the Cheek

This gesture signifies genuine interest and that a person is evaluating things in their mind while listening to your offer. It is, therefore, useful to ask questions or solicit ideas to hear thoughts.

Chin Stroking

It is at this point when the other party could be making a decision, so try not to interrupt! Look out instead for the next cue as when the person leans back and crosses their arms. These are negative gestures which mean a big NO!

Draw points of agreement and clarify any disagreement. However, if the person leans forward, keep silent and allow them to talk.

Seated Readiness

This indicates excitement and agreement. If followed by stroking of the chin, it's as good as saying YES! At this point, use the word "we" to point out that you're both in agreement.

Head Tilted

When the head is tilted, it means the person is showing interest in whatever it is you're offering. You may use these gestures to show interest and create a perception of being a good listener.

Tell-Tale Signs of Disagreement

There are negative nonverbal signs to show that the person disagrees with you or is simply hostile. It's best to read the person's gestures in a cluster than read a single cue to avoid misreading the message conveyed by their body language.

Crossed Arms

Generally, this move is an indication of being defensive. It doesn't mean that the person simply shut themselves off from any discussion or listening to any of it. It's just a matter of filtering everything being heard that affects the other person. According to Gerald I Nierenberger who wrote the book, *How to Read a Person Like A Book,* in a study involving more than 2000 negotiations, not one was closed when negotiating participants had arms and legs crossed during the negotiation. For those with participants who have negotiators with opened arms and legs, they were able to reach a deal.

Hand Supporting the Chin

This gesture implies boredom and has no interest whatsoever on what is being discussed. When this gesture is combined with vacant nods and glazed eyes, it means you indeed have lost connection with your audience. It could be that your speech is too long it, your audience is bored, or you're giving to many details that simply didn't interest your listener. Try to be direct in your negotiation. Remember that businesspeople have little time to spare and most of the time, their minds are busy somewhere else, so you need to prove yourself interesting.

To test if the person is still with you, stop talking. This can make the other person jump in and move on to something else. Sometimes, boredom can be a result of your talking more about yourself than the deal itself.

Chapter 11: Is Faking Body Language Possible?

Can you learn body language and acquire it as a skill?

Can you fake your body language?

It is possible for you to learn the common body language but according to new studies, there is a whole new set of cues that, if not possible, could be difficult to control.

Through being conscious and careful repetition, one can be more confident and easily learn some of this body language:

- Keep your hands out of your pockets.
- To remain open and honest, use your hands expressively.
- Keep your hands away from your face.

Microexpressions

Microexpressions are simple facial expressions that may happen in a split second and momentarily reveal your emotions. Microexpressions or micro signals are helpful so that you may be able to discern a liar from an honest person. These may range from a frown, furrow, wrinkles, smirk, or a smile. These serve as a fleeting glimpse into a person's inner feelings.

The frontalis, risorius and corrugator muscles are responsible for the appearance of microexpressions. They are stimulated by your emotions and almost impossible to control consciously. Let's take the fake smile as an example. A fake smile is an expression that we use in order to show someone that we are happy even if we really are not. Fake smiles are easily detected when given attention because though the lip muscles are pulled across your mouth to form a smile, the muscles controlling the eyes do not go together and play their part.

Researchers use specialized computer software to detect micro signals. They use computers so they can catch the fleeting facial expression that happens so fast that it is almost impossible for another human to pick up consciously.

High-speed cameras may also be used. By slowing down videos, repeating and observing them carefully, you may be able to detect microexpressions.

It may be difficult to detect and control microexpressions but the fact is, at some levels, the ability to detect and understand them has evolved. You must not underestimate microexpressions because it can simply betray your inward emotions in a blink of an eye and can be detected by good observers. Never assume that you can easily fake your way in conversations or even without speaking because these minute actions say a lot about your true emotions.

You might notice times when you meet a person and have a feeling that that person can't be trusted. It may be that your subconscious intuition is at work and gives you the feeling of mistrust towards that person that you couldn't formulate into words. The reason behind that is the combination of your intuition and micro-signals that you picked up from the person.

You might encounter researchers who say that the part of the body easiest to control is the face. This is not absolutely true as you can find circumstances in which the result is contrary to that statement.

A good example of that is the botox treatment in which the facial muscles are injected with low-level toxins so as to avoid wrinkles from appearing. If facial muscles are the easiest to control, why can't we just avoid using these muscles so that we won't have wrinkles when we age? It's because it's not that just as simple as we think. If the majority of our muscles are under our deliberate control, we'll just focus on controlling these muscles and we'll not be able to focus on other things that are of more importance.

Another example is about speech control. Notice whenever we speak there are appropriate gestures and facial expressions that go along with it. Did you ever try expressing your deepest feelings with other people but at the same time, you are controlling your face muscles contrary to the feeling that you need to portray? Or you remain poker-faced despite overflowing emotions while you speak out? Facial expressions are our natural response to whatever is happening around us. It is closely connected to our emotions and thoughts. It enables us to identify the precise feelings of the portrayer and that's why we rely on reading it most of the time.

Another way to detect insincerity is through observing incongruent body language. It means that what you say is inconsistent with what you are doing. Women are experts in this area because they have the ability to perceive the whole picture and can identify obscurities and artifices in persons and circumstances faster than men. Also, according to some researches, women can perform multiple tasks at once.

Oftentimes, you will hear women say their senses tingle when they feel that something isn't right (female intuition). The good thing is that men can also develop this skill through practice.

Chapter 12: Training Exercises to Improve Body Language

Your body language—your posture, gestures, position, and facial expressions—affects the people around you and even your own emotions. This works vice versa; that is, their body language also influences yours.

Whether we like or not, emotions motivate all of us. One of the best ways to enhance that drive is to improve your body language. Sooner or later, the change that started from you will reverberate to those around you, resulting in an overall change in your environment.

Most of us can't directly change our emotions but we can definitely change our body language in order to upgrade our lifestyle. This chapter introduces training exercising that would help enhance your nonverbal behavior.

Body Language Exercises (Solo)

This simple exercise is intended for you to get know your own nonverbal behavior including your facial expressions and body language.

Instructions

- Talk, walk and act in front of your mirror (preferably a full-length mirror).
- Take a candid video of yourself then review it. Give appropriate feedback regarding your body language in a given situation.
- Pick up a good habit (e.g. observing proper posture) or unlearn a bad one (e.g. pointing your finger at someone or putting your hands inside your pockets). Consistently practice this new habit until it becomes imprinted in you.
- Ask a close friend or your family to observe you and pinpoint the body language you need to work on in order to improve.

Many individuals find public speaking intimidating. They feel nervous to be exposed to a lot of people and vulnerable to criticism in the process. Simply put, they lack the confidence to face others. However, research shows that you can trick your emotions using your own body language. For instance, you can convince yourself that you feel happy when you keep on smiling. This is the same as the feeling of confidence during public speaking. Improving your posture, gestures, and facial expressions will help you confidently face and speak even to a myriad of people.

For this exercise, it would help to practice in a vacant, open-spaced area or you can start doing this at home. This is also to be carried out several days (or weeks if you must) before your public speaking engagement.

Instructions

- Think of the most common facial expressions, gestures, and body language associated with positive emotions.
- Stand in the vacant area and visualize a setting wherein you are standing before the members of the board, students, or a VIP.
- Relax your body, distributing your weight on both your feet. As you do this, think of these assertions in order to positively condition your mind: I feel great. I am cool. I can do this. I am the best!
- Square your shoulders, straighten your back, relax your arms at your sides, and begin to confidently walk forward as you recite your mantra with confidence. If it helps, you can speak the mantra out loud. Once you've reached the other end of the area (or your room), turn around and continue to walk with the same attitude. Continue to practice this every day.

- Bring the challenge up to another level by going to a busy part of the town and walking the way you have been practicing (without reciting the mantra out loud, of course). Repeat this confidence exercise and don't be afraid to grab various opportunities when you can show the results of this exercise.

Your body language tells a lot of things about you. When it speaks confidence and reliability, many people would be drawn to you and as they say, people always introduce opportunities. This exercise aims to help you develop the body language of a leader.

Instructions

- Begin with your posture. People's attention is often drawn by someone with good posture—whether standing, walking or sitting. Posture often reflects your inner state of mind. People with a positive outlook in life often carry themselves with confidence, that is with the back straight and chest out. Always check yourself to see if you are stooping or slouching.

- Release your tension and inhibitions. Get rid of the tension in your neck, shoulder, jaw, and tongue by putting two fingertips in your mouth right under your tongue then slowly releasing them. Remember, your tongue should be relaxed during the process. It shouldn't appear concave, convex or too tensed. Put your other hand under your lip line, creating a V between your index finger and thumb. Gently pull your jaw down to about half to one inch. Observe yourself in the mirror and see how your tongue might pull back or your neck and shoulders become tense. Do this exercise regularly and you will feel more relaxed and confident over time.
- Make sure that your gestures are purposeful. Gestures put power and emphasis on your message so it's advisable

not to overuse them. They shouldn't just be random, repetitive or unintentional. You can practice them as you speak in front of the mirror. Observe how each gesture visually intensifies or abates a word or a sentence in your speech.

- Work on your handshake since it is the first connection you make with another person. In the eyes of the third party, it may look like a simple greeting gesture, but it actually says a lot. A handshake serves as an equalizer and tells the sincerity and warmth of a person. A lousy and fleeting handshake or an aggressive one puts you in a disadvantage. On the other hand, a firm and sincere handshake helps establish trust. Maintain eye contact while shaking hands and never rush.

Body Language Exercises (Group Activity)

This exercise helps illustrate relevant points on body language. The participants are trained to readily understand a particular mood based on the given nonverbal signals of a person. By identifying the signals, specifically the negative ones, the emotional contagion can be avoided. This is particularly helpful in the workplace where people are expected to improve their relationships by controlling and improving their body language.

Objective

To be aware of the different nonverbal signals and identify the mood behind them.

Needed Materials

"Emotion cards" with the following emotions depicted on them:

- Satisfied
- Bored
- Frustrated
- Impressed
- Traumatized
- Depressed

- Happy
- Confident
- Angry
- Nervous
- Stressed
- Cynical
- Agitated
- Unconvinced
- Peaceful
- Scared
- Surprised
- Disgusted

Timing

Explaining the exercise: 2 minutes

Activity: 10 minutes

Discussion: 5-10 minutes

Instructions

- The facilitator should ask for a volunteer who will enact the emotion stated on the given emotion card.
- The participants should sit at one side of the room. The volunteer will then stand in front of the participants and proceed to act out what was written in the card.
- The participants should guess the emotion and proceed to discuss the body language used to portray it.
- Repeat the process until everybody has been given the chance to perform in front.

Questions for the Group Discussion

- How easy was it to enact and give the corresponding body language based on the emotions in the emotion card?
- How would you feel when confronted by the person with negative emotions such as anger, fear, disgust, etc.?

- Were there times when you felt your own mood changed based on the (negative or positive) body language exhibited by a certain person in your workplace or at home?
- When someone was depressed or stressed out, did you feel the same way, too?
- How can you control your own emotions or negative nonverbal behavior in order to avoid affecting other people?

Objective

Identify nonverbal cues and explain the meaning behind these signals by observing the people in various situations as portrayed in the images or videos.

Needed Materials

Set of images or video clips showing various people in daily situations based on these ideas:

- People during a board meeting
- A teacher during his or her class

- Two individuals greeting each other
- People while waiting in a subway station, airport, etc.
- A politician during an interview or press conference
- An individual during a public plea regarding a missing family member or relative

Timing

Explaining the exercise: 2 minutes

Activity: 10-20 minutes

Discussion: 5-10 minutes

Instructions

- Each participant should be able to take notes based on what they see or observe in each image or video presentation, paying closer attention to facial expressions, body language, posture, and other nonverbal behavior.

- Each participant should be able to share their notes.
- Encourage discussion based on the participants' different opinions.
- Questions for the group discussion.
- How easy was it to understand and interpret nonverbal communication?
- Was there a pattern in common postures, gestures or tone of voice for a particular emotion?
- Do you think the people in the images or videos were conscious about their body language during that certain time?
- What is the importance of understanding body language?
- Which areas should you focus on learning the most?

Some people are really fast talkers, talking at the same pace as we think. Because of this, they can't help but to mumble short sentences and skip words, making what they say sound incoherent.

Although they are smart, others think that they're quite the opposite.

This exercise is designed for fast talkers to help them improve their diction and gain confidence by eloquently expressing themselves.

Objective

Help participants to talk at an ideal speed and also allow them to express what they're saying using various gestures and nonverbal cues.

Time

Explaining the exercise: 5 minutes

Activity: 20 minutes (10 minutes per round)

Group Discussion: 10 minutes

Instructions

- Working in pairs, the participants should choose who will be the talker and the imitator. Talkers will be those who are going to choose a subject they will talk about. They can talk about everything like their experience in their previous vacation, everyday work experience, a Caribbean adventure, their high school adventure or about a story they read about.

- While the talkers tell about their stories, the imitators will act out what they hear using various gestures and body language. This method helps both parties in two important areas: First, the talkers are forced to talk at a slower pace so that the imitators will have the time to understand and enact what they say. Secondly, the imitators are forced to concentrate on what the talkers have to tell so they can express it accordingly.
- After ten minutes, the partners should switch roles and perform the exercise for another ten minutes.
- Gather everyone for a group discussion.

Questions for the Group Discussion

- How can you assess your talking speed? Did the exercise help you slow it down?
- Do you think you can adjust your speed next time even without your imitator?

The exercise aims to help you identify various nonverbal cues and realize how these signals affect the way you communicate with other people. You get trained on how to understand the importance of communication in a given social context without using words. Moreover, this exercise helps you enhance your writing creativity.

Objective

Write a short story that should be carried out using body language.

Needed Materials

- Pen
- Paper

Time

Explaining the exercise: 5 minutes

Creating the dialogue: 30 minutes

Performance: 5 minutes per group

Group Discussion: 10 minutes

Instructions

- Working in pairs, discuss and write down a 600-word dialogue within 30 minutes. Make sure that each line can be acted out using gestures, facial expressions, and body language.
- The narrator (the facilitator) will then read the story or dialogue and the pair of actors will proceed to act out their lines using body language.
- The audience (those who are not yet performing) should be able to provide feedback after each story.
- After every pair is finished, call for a group discussion.

Questions for the Group Discussion

- What was your first impression when you were asked to create a story/ dialogue? Did you think that it's going to be challenging?
- Did you find writing the story/ dialogue hard? What's the difficulty of the task?
- How did you find acting or communicating through body language? Was it easy or difficult?
- How does this exercise improve your nonverbal expressions?

Objective

Write a story or dialogue, design characters, and act it out.

Needed Materials

- Time Pen
- Paper (A4)

Time

- Explaining the exercise: 5 minutes
- Part 1 Writing and planning activity: 20 minutes
- Part 2 Writing and planning activity: 20 minutes
- Part 3 Presentation: (role play discussion) 10 minutes and (actual presentation) 5 minutes per group
- Post Presentation Feedback: 5 minutes after each presentation
- Group Discussion: 10 minutes

Instructions

Part 1

The participants should be divided into three groups. Ask each group to design two characters. They can get ideas from the people they know or get inspiration from characters in popular movies, TV series, or novels.

The participants should write their character sketches in an A4-sized paper using a narrative description. Each sketch should tell who the character is without having it say or do anything (Note: Each character sketch should not exceed one A4-sized paper.) Work on the sketch for 20 minutes.

Part 2

Each group should pass their character sketch to the group on their left. This time, each group should take time to study and understand the character sketches they received. They are discouraged to discuss the sketches with the original group who made the sketch or with other groups.

The groups should use the characters in a scenario or a story. They should write a dramatic dialogue between the two characters. In the scene, each character should have a secret they cannot divulge with each other, not even to the audience (Note: The dialogue should not exceed two A4-sized papers.) Work on the dialogue for 20 minutes.

Part 3

The groups should pass the dialogue they made (but not the character sketches) to the group on their left. They need to review and understand the dialogue and select two of their members to act out the story in front of the whole class. Allow 10 minutes for them to talk about their plans for the role play.

Each group should present their skit for about 5 minutes per presentation. The actors should be able to effectively express their characters using various gestures, facial expressions, and body language.

After each presentation, the viewers are allowed to give comments on the character design, dialogues, and the actual presentation.

Proceed with the general discussion after the presentations.

Questions for the Group Discussion

- What are your opinions about the process of designing the characters?
- What can you say about the process of creating the dialogues based on the character sketches?
- (To the actors) How do you find the process of acting out the characters based on the dialogues?
- What gestures, facial expressions, or body language are used to support or define the given traits of each character in the story?

This exercise helps the participants to understand and recognize the power of making eye contact as it can affect emotional connection and relationship between people, particularly in the work setting.

Objective

Establish the habit of making eye contact, thus, helping the participants develop positive body language

Needed Materials

- Blank cards or index cards for easy writing while standing
- Pen

Timing

Explaining the exercise: 5 minutes

Activity (Stages 1-2): 5 minutes

Group Discussion: 10 minutes

Instructions

Stage 1

The participants should freely roam the room like they were in the public place and they don't know each other. They are not yet encouraged to establish eye contact this time. Do this for about a minute.

After the allotted time, ask them to stop and write down how they felt during that time.

Stage 2

The participants should try making eye contact with each other as they go about the room but they should immediately break it and look away. Allow this for two minutes.

Again, stop everyone and let them write down how they felt during those two minutes.

Stage 3

For this round, ask the participants to establish eye contact and as soon as they do this, they should pair up together. They should stand together at a particular spot in the room, refusing to make eye contact with the rest of the group for two minutes.

After two minutes, the participants should write down how they felt.

End this activity and call for a group discussion.

Questions for the Group Discussion

- How did you feel during the various stages of the activity?
- How did you feel when you didn't have to make eye contact with the people around you?
- How did you feel when you needed to break the eye contact right away?
- How did you feel when you established eye contact and had to pair up with your partner?
- Did you immediately find someone you could pair up with? If not, how did you feel about it?
- What kind of preconditioning triggers our behavior in trying to make eye contact and maintaining it?

- How does this simple practice differ in various societies all around the globe? Cite different examples of this.

Conclusion

Acquiring skills related to understanding, reading, and analyzing nonverbal communication or body language can be useful in itself. It's a handy tool that gives you the edge over others as you can use it to improve all aspects of your life – personal, relationships, career, and business.

Mastering this skill can help you communicate and understand other people and the messages they want to convey other than the use of words. It can be a lot of fun knowing what other people are thinking, especially when they are lying, and how comfortable they are in a given situation.

That said, the nonverbal cues we are trying to interpret are not going to tell us 100 percent what the other person is feeling or thinking. However, once you find clues that will help you understand other people better, you can use them to communicate effectively as you gain more awareness of those around you. All you need to do is pay more attention to people's actions, movements, and reactions as you, likewise, become more sensitive to your natural human intuition blended with logic and reason.

www.ingramcontent.com/pod-product-compliance
Lightning Source LLC
Chambersburg PA
CBHW030108100526
44591CB00009B/321